PANORAMA

A HISTORY OF

FLIGHT

FROM BALLOONS TO BOEINGS

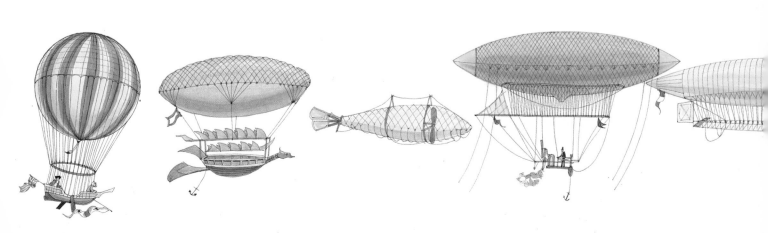

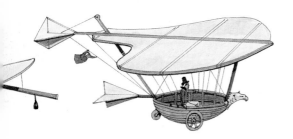

Author:
Peter Lafferty is a former secondary school science teacher. Since 1985 he has been a full-time author of science and technology books for children and family audiences. He has written 50 books and contributed to many well-known encyclopedias. He has also edited scientific encyclopedias and dictionaries. He lives in Sussex and when not writing books or walking his dog, he can usually be found fishing for trout.

Series designer:
David Salariya was born in Dundee, Scotland, where he studied illustration and printmaking, concentrating on book design in his post-graduate year. He later completed a further post-graduate course in art education at Sussex University. He has illustrated a wide range of books on botanical, historical and mythical subjects. He has designed and created many new series of children's books for publishers in the UK and overseas, including the award-winning **Inside Story** series. He lives in Brighton with his wife, the illustrator Shirley Willis.

Artist:
Mark Bergin studied illustration at Eastbourne College of Art. Since leaving art school in 1983, he has specialised in illustrating books on historical, architectural and technological subjects. He lives in Sussex with his wife and family.

Series designer: David Salariya
Editor: Penny Clarke
Artist: Mark Bergin

First published in 1996
by Macdonald Young Books
61 Western Road
Hove
East Sussex
BN3 1JD

ISBN 0-7500-1748-1

© The Salariya Book Co Ltd MCMXCVI

Printed in Portugal by Ediçoes ASA

A CIP catalogue record for this book is available from the British Library title page copy

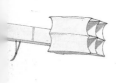

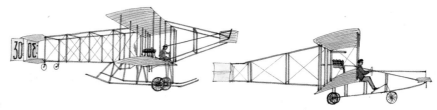

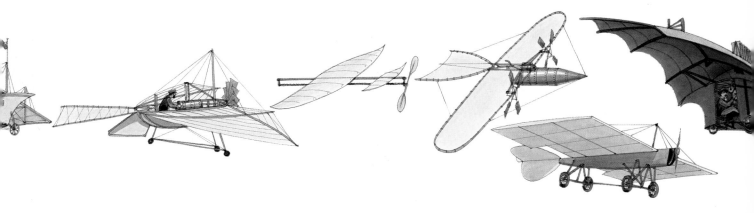

PANORAMA
A HISTORY OF
FLIGHT
FROM BALLOONS TO BOEINGS

Written by
PETER LAFFERTY

Created & Designed by
DAVID SALARIYA

Illustrated by
MARK BERGIN

MACDONALD YOUNG BOOKS

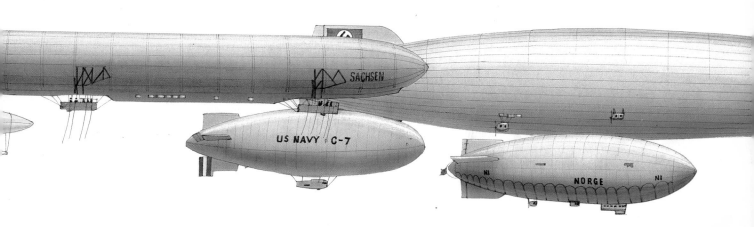

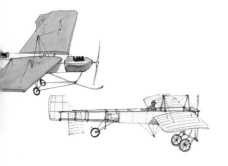
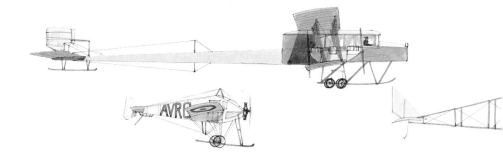

Contents

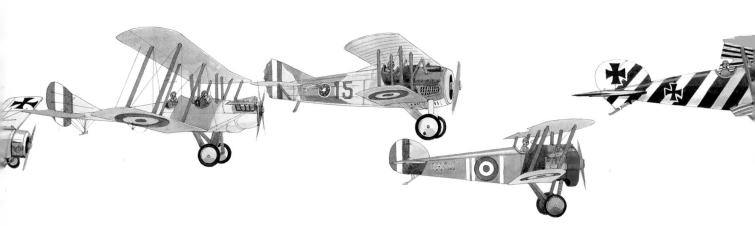

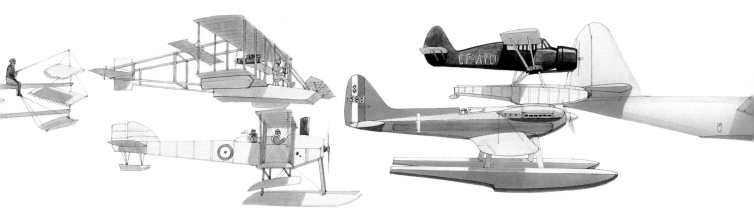

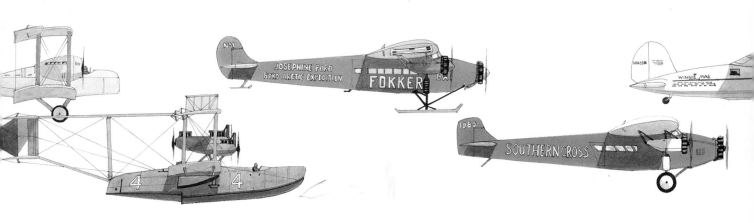

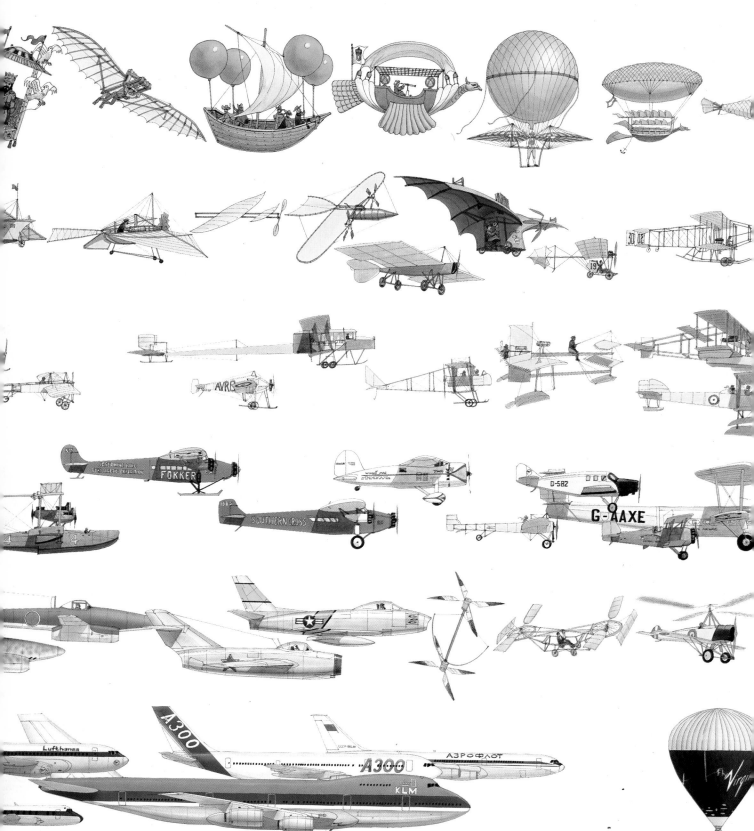

INTRODUCTION

People have always dreamed of being able to fly. The ancient Greeks told of Daedalus and Icarus who escaped from prison on the island of Crete by flying. They were said to have fixed feathers to their arms with wax to make wings. Icarus came to grief when the wax melted as he flew too close to the sun. This, and other similar legends, tempted foolish people to jump from towers with feathers on their arms. Naturally, they plummetted to the ground and were killed. It is not so easy to fly.

Two things are needed for sustained flight: a

light and powerful engine to lift the aircraft and a way of controlling the craft once it is in the air. The Wright brothers, Wilbur and Orville, were the first to discover this. In 1903 they made the first sustained flight at Kitty Hawk, North Carolina, USA. Since then, aviation progress has been rapid. Planes can now carry hundreds of passengers at a time, fly non-stop around the world, and exceed the speed of sound.

Even the dream of human-powered flight has come true. In 1988, Kanellos Kanellopoulos, a Greek cyclist, flew from Crete to a nearby island, entirely under his own power, in a machine called *Daedalus* after the Greek hero.

7

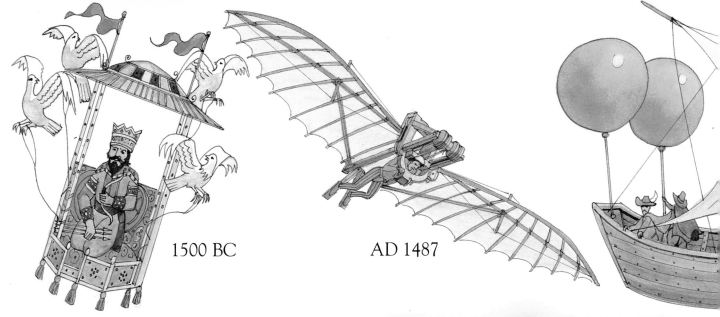

1500 BC

AD 1487

FLIGHTS OF FANCY

According to legend, Bladud, King of England in the 9th century BC, jumped from a high building wearing a pair of wings. He crashed to his death.

Have you ever wished that you could fly? If you have, you are not alone. People have longed to soar like the birds since the earliest times. In the Bible, the psalmist David cried, 'Oh that I had wings like a dove! for then would I fly away, and be at rest.'

The gods of ancient people were often thought to have wings. After all, the gods could travel anywhere and everywhere and what better way was there than flying. Ordinary people, when they first attempted to fly, tried to imitate birds. So began the story of 'bird men' who jumped off towers, flapping their feathered arms.

Other, slightly more realistic schemes were put forward over the centuries but none achieved flight. Leonardo da Vinci realized that human muscle power was insufficient for flight. He designed flying machines that used levers and pulleys to overcome this difficulty, but his machines never got off the ground.

The first hint of how flight might be achieved came in 1709 when a Jesuit priest, Laurenço de Gusmão, demonstrated a small model to the King of Portugal. The model was lifted by hot air from a fire. Here, at last, was a lifting agent that might raise people off the ground.

IN THE ANCIENT WORLD, every nation had its winged gods. This example is from Egypt, but similar creatures were worshipped in China, Persia, Rome and South America.

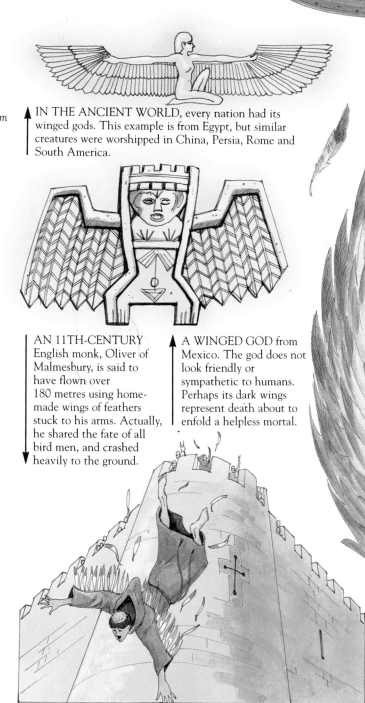

AN 11TH-CENTURY English monk, Oliver of Malmesbury, is said to have flown over 180 metres using home-made wings of feathers stuck to his arms. Actually, he shared the fate of all bird men, and crashed heavily to the ground.

A WINGED GOD from Mexico. The god does not look friendly or sympathetic to humans. Perhaps its dark wings represent death about to enfold a helpless mortal.

1670

1709

1800s

A WELL-KNOWN LEGEND from Greece tells how Daedalus and his son Icarus used wings made from feathers and wax to escape from imprisonment by Minos, King of Crete. During the flight, Daedalus warned Icarus not to fly too high, lest the heat of the sun melt the wax holding the feathers in place. But Icarus, elated by the experience of flight, rose higher and higher until his wings disintegrated. He fell into the sea and drowned. Daedelus flew on to reach safety in Sicily.

1500 BC Kai Kawus, King of Persia nearly 3,500 years ago, is said to have flown by harnessing four geese to a throne. Drawings of him in flight show that he travelled in considerable luxury. He carried a bow and arrow to defend himself from other aerial voyagers.

AD 1487 Italian scientist, artist and engineer, Leonardo da Vinci made a careful study of how birds fly. He became convinced that people would never fly using the muscles of their arms alone. He designed about 150 different flying machines with pulleys and levers to increase the pilot's muscle power.

1670 A priest, Francesco de Lana-Terzi, produced the first design for a lighter-than-air vehicle. It was intended to be lifted by four hollow copper spheres from which the air had been pumped. However, de Lana found that if the copper skins of the spheres were too thin, the spheres collapsed due to atmospheric pressure. If the spheres were thick enough to withstand the pressure, they were too heavy to fly.

1709 Father Laurenço de Gusmão made the first model craft to make a free flight. The model consisted of a small trough covered by a cloth. Oil was burned in the trough, producing hot air which was trapped under the cloth, lifting the craft. Gusmão is said to have made a full-size version, called the *Passarola* or *Great Bird*. It failed to fly.

1800s In the early 19th century, a Swiss watchmaker named Jacob Degan claimed to have flown in his aircraft with flapping wings. In fact, the craft only became airborne because it had a hot-air balloon attached.

1783

1785

1837

1850

First Flights by Balloon

Joseph Montgolfier, pioneer of the hot-air balloon.

The lifting power of hot air was first put to use by the Montgolfier brothers, Joseph and Etienne, in France. Joseph is said to have held a paper bag, open end downward, over a fire. When he released the bag, it floated to the ceiling. This led the brothers to experiment with larger and larger bags. On 4 June, 1783, they gave a public demonstration in which a paper-lined linen bag, 11 metres in diameter, rose to 1,800 metres. Later in the same year they sent animals and humans aloft in balloons.

One problem with the early balloons was that, relying on hot air, they had to be huge to lift a useful weight. Greater lift was provided by hydrogen gas, discovered by English chemist Henry Cavendish in 1766. Jacques Charles used hydrogen in an unmanned balloon on 27 August, 1783.

Another problem was that the early balloons were difficult to control. Henri Giffard partly solved this problem with his streamlined steam-powered airship in 1852. However, it was not until 1884 – over 100 years after the first balloon flights – that a fully controllable airship took to the air.

THE FIRST LIVING CREATURES to fly in a hot-air balloon were a sheep, a cock and a duck. In September 1783, they were sent aloft in a balloon (left) by the Montgolfier brothers to see if they could breathe in the rarified air high above the ground. They survived, although the cock broke a wing, probably because it was kicked by the sheep. Encouraged by this success, Jean-François Pilâre de Rozier ascended to 25 metres in a balloon in October 1783. On 21 November, 1783, de Rozier and the Marquis d'Arlandes travelled 9 kilometres across Paris in a balloon (right). The Marquis had the job of stoking the fire that produced the hot air that kept the balloon airborne. The fire burned in the brazier that hung beneath the open neck of the balloon. The Marquis also had to put out any flames with a wet sponge if the balloon caught fire.

THE FIRST parachute descent was made by Frenchman Louis Lenormand in 1783. He jumped from a tree and then from a tower in the town of Montpellier. André Garnerin made the first public demonstration of a parachute descent (right) from a balloon in Paris in 1797.

10

1852

1884

1783 French professor Jacques Charles made the first flight in a hydrogen-filled balloon on 1 December, 1783. On an earlier trial flight, local farmers had attacked his balloon with pitchforks, believing it to be the work of the devil.

1785 The first balloon flight across the English Channel almost ended in disaster. The balloonists were American John Jeffries and Frenchman Jean-Pierre Blanchard. The balloon leaked badly and the pilots were forced to throw everything they could overboard. This saved the day and the balloon landed safely in a forest near Calais, France.

1837 Sir George Cayley, an English aristocrat, first suggested that the gas bags of balloons should be made streamlined to increase control. He designed a craft, called an airship, which had steam-driven propellers. It was never built.

1850 Frenchman Pierre Jullien built a model airship which was streamlined as suggested by George Cayley. It was named the *Précurseur* and was propelled by a clockwork-driven propeller.

1852 Frenchman Henri Giffard made the first flight in his streamlined hydrogen-filled airship in 1852. A steam engine turned a propeller to drive it along. It carried its inventor 27 kilometres from Paris to Trappes.

1884 The first completely controllable airship was the electrically-powered *La France*, built by Charles Renard and Arthur Krebs in 1884. The craft was big, with a length of 50 metres. It was also fast, with a top speed of 22 km/h.

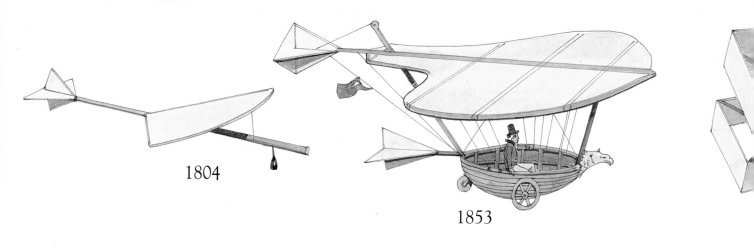

1804

1853

Gliding Through the Air

The Chinese built kites over 2,000 years ago. They may even have built passenger-carrying ones. Kites were first flown in Europe in the 1300s.

A round 1800, an English aristocrat, Sir George Cayley, had first begun to wonder if a large kite-like machine might be able to carry passengers. In 1804, he built a model glider which flew reasonably well. He wrote in his notebook: 'It was very pretty to see it sail down a steep hill, and it gave the idea that a larger instrument would be a better and safer conveyance down the Alps than even a sure-footed mule.' By 1809 he had built a full-sized glider which was tested with a boy on board.

The next great aviation pioneer was the German Otto Lilienthal. He built gliders which were similar to modern hang-gliders. He covered distances of more than 225 metres, up to 22 metres above the ground. Unfortunately, in 1896 he lost control of a glider and crashed. He broke his spine and died the next day. His last words were 'Sacrifices must be made'.

Lilienthal's efforts inspired other aviators, such as Percy Pilcher in England and Octave Chanute in America, to experiment with gliders. Gradually, glider design was improved until the time came to try fitting an engine.

GERMAN OTTO LILIENTHAL made hundreds of glider flights between 1891 and 1896. He hung beneath his gliders and swung his body around to control the flight. He built both monoplanes (with one wing) and biplanes (with two wings).

IN THE 1890s, Australian Lawrence Hargrave designed several passenger-carrying box kites.

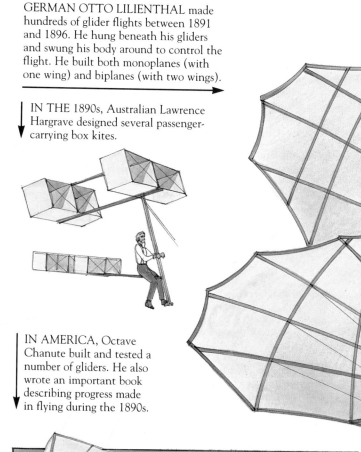

IN AMERICA, Octave Chanute built and tested a number of gliders. He also wrote an important book describing progress made in flying during the 1890s.

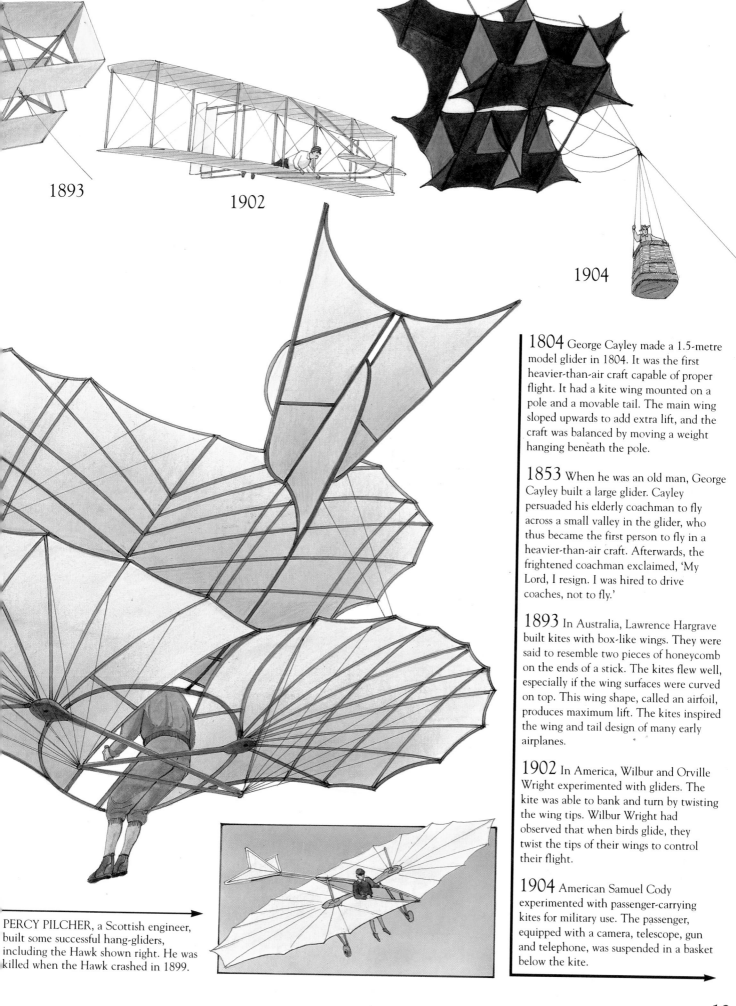

1893

1902

1904

1804 George Cayley made a 1.5-metre model glider in 1804. It was the first heavier-than-air craft capable of proper flight. It had a kite wing mounted on a pole and a movable tail. The main wing sloped upwards to add extra lift, and the craft was balanced by moving a weight hanging beneath the pole.

1853 When he was an old man, George Cayley built a large glider. Cayley persuaded his elderly coachman to fly across a small valley in the glider, who thus became the first person to fly in a heavier-than-air craft. Afterwards, the frightened coachman exclaimed, 'My Lord, I resign. I was hired to drive coaches, not to fly.'

1893 In Australia, Lawrence Hargrave built kites with box-like wings. They were said to resemble two pieces of honeycomb on the ends of a stick. The kites flew well, especially if the wing surfaces were curved on top. This wing shape, called an airfoil, produces maximum lift. The kites inspired the wing and tail design of many early airplanes.

1902 In America, Wilbur and Orville Wright experimented with gliders. The kite was able to bank and turn by twisting the wing tips. Wilbur Wright had observed that when birds glide, they twist the tips of their wings to control their flight.

1904 American Samuel Cody experimented with passenger-carrying kites for military use. The passenger, equipped with a camera, telescope, gun and telephone, was suspended in a basket below the kite.

PERCY PILCHER, a Scottish engineer, built some successful hang-gliders, including the Hawk shown right. He was killed when the Hawk crashed in 1899.

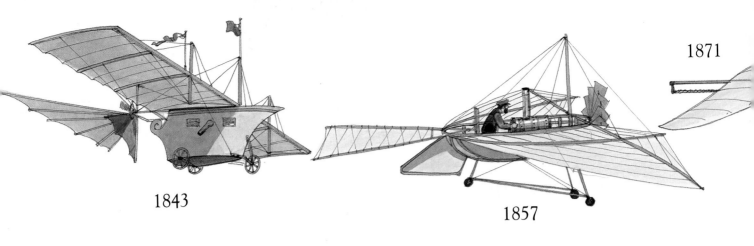

1871

1843

1857

THE FIRST POWERED HOPS

The first airplanes with engines could not fly properly; the steam engines used were too heavy and did not have enough power. However, a few pioneers did persuade their steam-powered craft to hop a short distance into the air. The first airplane to take off and fly under its own power was built by a French naval officer, Felix du Temple. In 1874, du Temple built a steam-powered plane which managed a short hop after gathering speed down a steep slope. The first full-sized airplane to take off from level ground was the *Ecole*, a bat-winged craft built by Clement Ader in France. In 1890, the *Ecole* managed a 50-metre hop.

In 1896, Samuel Pierpoint Langley, an American professor, built a large model aircraft, with a 4.8-metre wing-span, powered by a steam engine. It flew for 0.8 kilometre. Encouraged, Langley then turned to the petrol engine to power his planes. He built a full-size craft called the *Aerodrome* which had a petrol engine. The *Aerodrome* was launched from a specially equipped houseboat on the Potomac River but crashed. Nevertheless, the light and powerful petrol engine was to prove the key to successful flight.

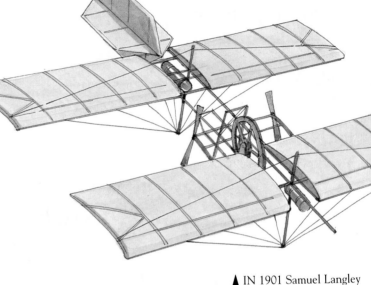

IN 1901 Samuel Langley made a quarter-scale model of the *Aerodrome*. This was the first machine ever to fly with a petrol engine. However Langley ignored the vital fact that his aircraft could not be controlled in flight.

FELIX DU TEMPLE'S steam-powered airplane of 1874 became airborne after travelling down a ramp, but it dropped to the ground almost at once. This probably saved du Temple's life, because he had no way of controlling the craft in flight.

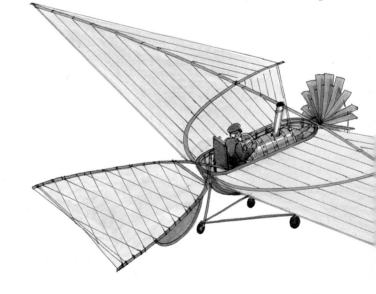

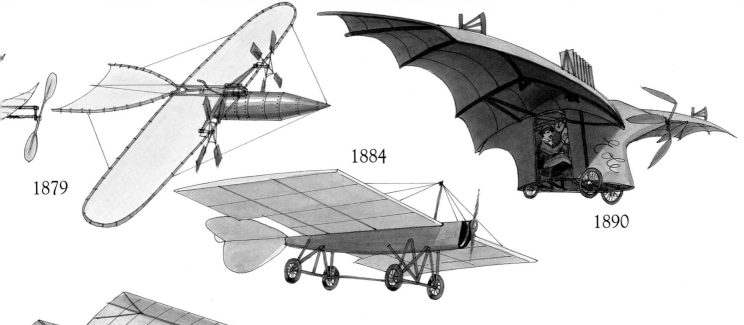

1879

1884

1890

1843 The first design for a steam-powered plane was made by Englishman William Henson, following the principles set down by George Cayley. Henson made a 6-metre model of his Aerial Steam Carriage, but it failed to fly because there was no suitable engine.

1857 Felix du Temple designed an aircraft in 1857 which had the propeller at the front, the best possible position. He made a model powered, at first, by a clockwork motor and later by a steam engine. This became the first heavier-than-air craft to take off and fly under its own power.

1871 Frenchman Alphonse Penaud started a craze for model aircraft in 1871. He did it with a simple craft called the Planophore with a front propeller powered by a twisted rubber band. He designed a full-size craft in 1876 but it was never built.

1879 In France, Victor Tatin built a successful model aircraft in 1879 which confirmed that the best layout was with the propeller at the front, a large front wing and a rear tail. His model was powered by compressed air.

1884 In Russia, a big steam-powered monoplane built by Alexander Mozhaisky made a short, ramp-assisted hop in 1884. The craft had broad wings, stretching along the complete length of the body.

1890 French engineer Clement Ader made a short flight in his bat-winged *Ecole*. The secret of his success was a light and efficient steam engine. However, the pilot had no way of controlling the craft.

SAMUEL LANGLEY'S full-sized aircraft, *Aerodrome*, was launched by catapult from a houseboat in 1903. The craft hit a post on the catapult gear as it was launched and plunged into the river (right). A second attempt later the same year suffered the same fate. Disappointed, Langley gave up his aviation experiments. Eleven years later, in 1914, Glenn Curtiss, another American aircraft designer, flew the *Aerodrome* successfully. However by then the Wright brothers had established their place in history as the creators of the practical airplane.

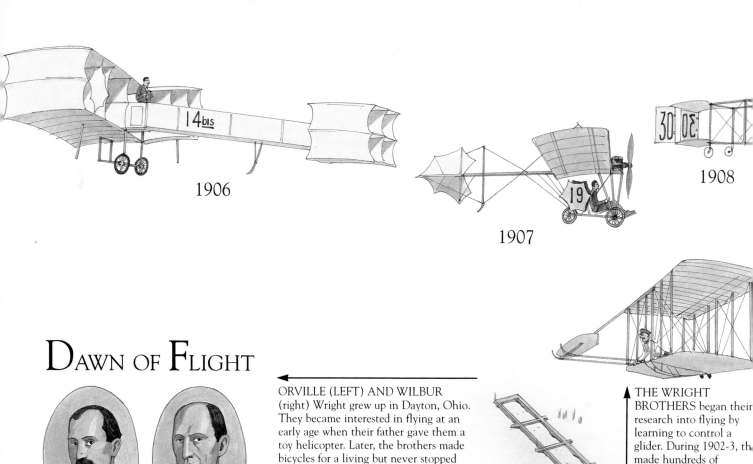

1906

1907

1908

Dawn of Flight

ORVILLE (LEFT) AND WILBUR (right) Wright grew up in Dayton, Ohio. They became interested in flying at an early age when their father gave them a toy helicopter. Later, the brothers made bicycles for a living but never stopped thinking about the problems of flight. After their success with *Flyer*, they continued to make airplanes until Wilbur died of typhoid fever in 1912. Orville died in 1948.

THE WRIGHT BROTHERS began their research into flying by learning to control a glider. During 1902-3, th[ey] made hundreds of successful glider flights.

On 17 December, 1903, at Kitty Hawk in North Carolina, USA, Orville Wright lay across the wings of a primitive aircraft, grasping its controls. His brother Wilbur ran alongside, gripping one wing to keep the craft steady as it moved along a launching rail. The biplane, called *Flyer*, moved slowly forward and rose in the air. It reached a height of about 3 metres and travelled about 36 metres before plunging into the ground. The flight had lasted 12 seconds. This first short hop was the beginning of the age of flight.

The brothers received little publicity for their remarkable achievement because the newspapers did not believe they had achieved powered flight. In May 1904 they invited reporters to witness the first take-off of an improved machine, *Flyer No. 2*. Unfortunately, the new engine was faulty and the aircraft simply ran to the end of the launch rail and stopped. After this, the brothers spent three more years improving the design until they were able to stay airborne for 38 minutes. Now, the Wright brothers' plane was hailed as the greatest invention of the age. After this, other aviation pioneers in America and Europe set to work developing planes.

1908

1909

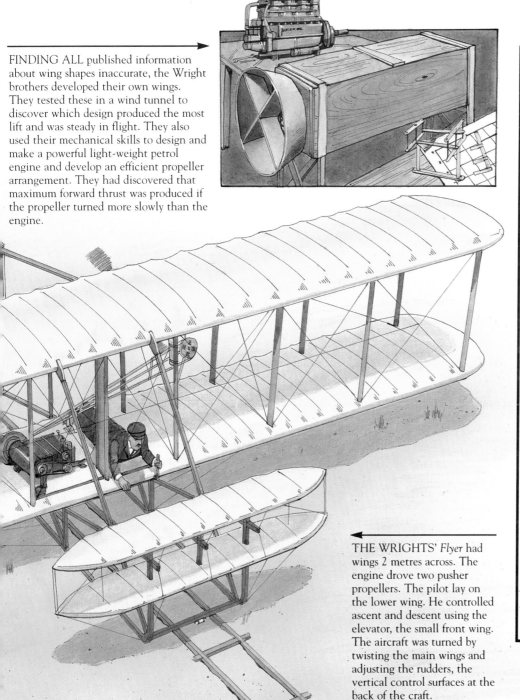

FINDING ALL published information about wing shapes inaccurate, the Wright brothers developed their own wings. They tested these in a wind tunnel to discover which design produced the most lift and was steady in flight. They also used their mechanical skills to design and make a powerful light-weight petrol engine and develop an efficient propeller arrangement. They had discovered that maximum forward thrust was produced if the propeller turned more slowly than the engine.

THE WRIGHTS' *Flyer* had wings 2 metres across. The engine drove two pusher propellers. The pilot lay on the lower wing. He controlled ascent and descent using the elevator, the small front wing. The aircraft was turned by twisting the main wings and adjusting the rudders, the vertical control surfaces at the back of the craft.

1906 Alberto Santos-Dumont was an outstanding European aviation pioneer. Born in Brazil but settled in Paris, he became famous when he flew an airship round the Eiffel Tower in 1901. Five years later, he made the first officially recognized airplane flight in Europe in his tail-first biplane. In doing so, he set a world air-speed record of 40 km/h.

1907 By 1907 Alberto Santos-Dumont had designed and built the tiny *Demoiselle*, intended as the first 'build-it-yourself' aircraft. At first unsuccessful, the *Demoiselle* became a practical craft two years later after many improvements.

1908 The world's first aircraft manufacturing company was set up in France by the Voisin brothers, Charles and Gabriel. One of their planes won a 50,000 franc prize in 1908 by flying in a circle of more than one kilometre in Europe.

1908 American Glenn Curtiss won a trophy by flying his *June Bug* for nearly 1.6 kilometres in 1908. This was the first officially observed flight in the United States. The *June Bug* was later developed into the *Gold Bug* which flew successfully at the 1909 Rheims air show.

1909 Alliott Verdon Roe was the greatest of the early British aircraft designers and pilots. His triplane (three-winged plane) was the first all-British aircraft to fly successfully. Short of money, Roe had to cover his triplane with brown paper.

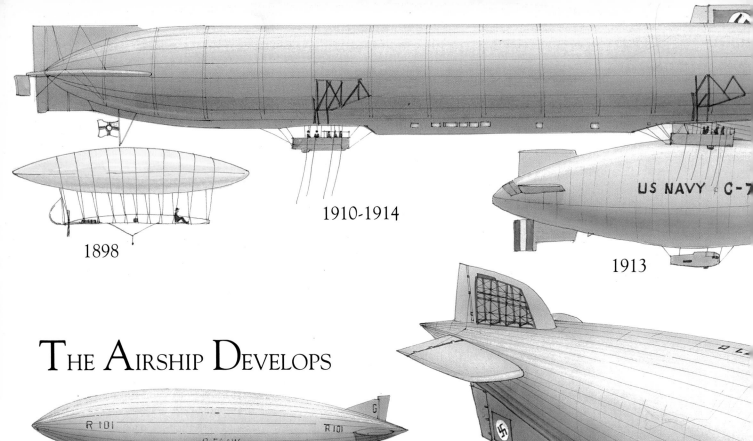

1910-1914

1898

US NAVY C-7

1913

THE AIRSHIP DEVELOPS

R 101   G

G-FAAW

R 101   G

The last British airship, the R101, crashed in 1930 killing 44 of the 54 crew and passengers.

D LZ 130

Early airships, driven by steam or electric motors, were under-powered. The Brazilian aviation pioneer, Alberto Santos-Dumont, solved this problem by combining the airship and the petrol engine. He built his first petrol-powered airship in 1898. Three years later, he flew an airship on an 11.3-kilometre journey, circling around the Eiffel Tower in Paris.

Santos-Dumont's airship was the 'non-rigid' type; its gas bag being kept in shape by the gas inside. This was not ideal as the bag could change shape and create drag. So a better type of airship, called a 'rigid', was developed. These new airships had gas containers inside a rigid metal framework, covered with cloth or thin metal. In Germany, Count Ferdinand Zeppelin began building these ships in 1900.

The first airlines used Zeppelin airships. After World War One, airships, such as the *Graf Zeppelin*, carried passengers across the Atlantic Ocean in about 3½ days. Later came the larger and even more luxurious *Hindenburg*. Alas, in 1937, this great airship burst into flames while being moored. Thirty-five people of the 97 people on board were killed.

THE AIRSHIP *Hindenburg* caught fire as it came in to land in Lakehurst, New Jersey, USA, on 6 May, 1937, after a flight of 62 hours. Within seconds, the *Hindenburg* was a blazing mass of wreckage. The cause of the explosion was the dangerous hydrogen gas used in the balloon. The hydrogen was probably ignited by static electricity as the airship approached the metal mooring mast after a thunderstorm. The explosion put an end to German plans to build a fleet of passenger airships. The British had decided to stop making large airships in 1930 after the *R101* had exploded.

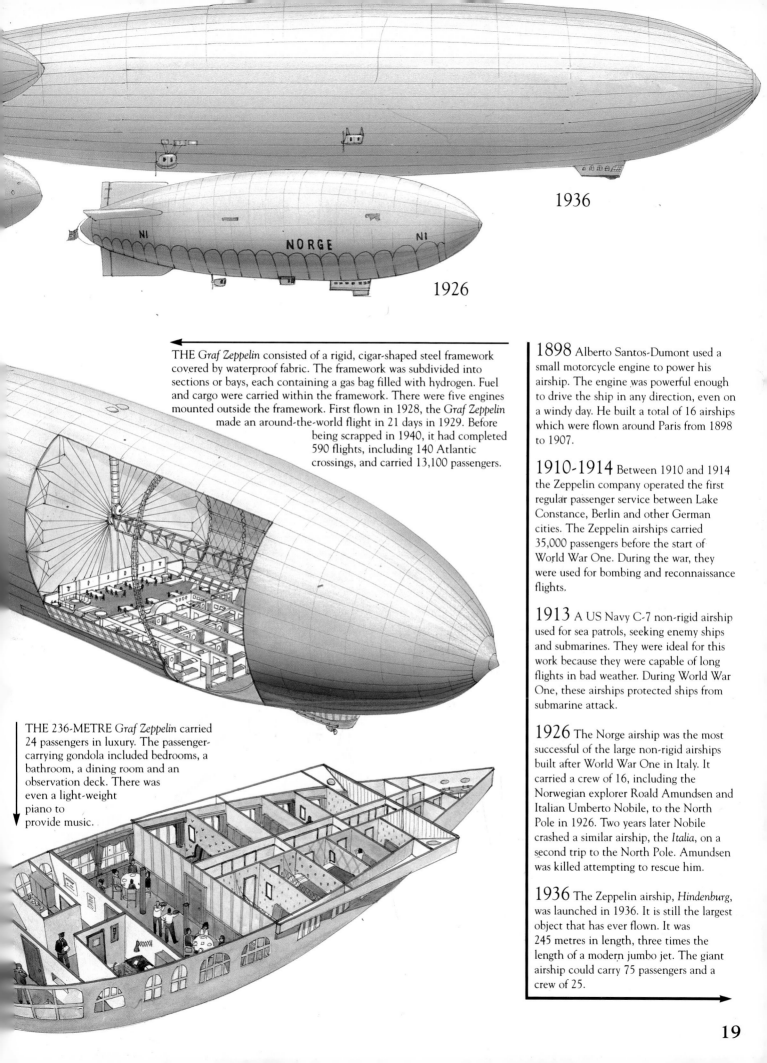

1936

1926

THE *Graf Zeppelin* consisted of a rigid, cigar-shaped steel framework covered by waterproof fabric. The framework was subdivided into sections or bays, each containing a gas bag filled with hydrogen. Fuel and cargo were carried within the framework. There were five engines mounted outside the framework. First flown in 1928, the *Graf Zeppelin* made an around-the-world flight in 21 days in 1929. Before being scrapped in 1940, it had completed 590 flights, including 140 Atlantic crossings, and carried 13,100 passengers.

THE 236-METRE *Graf Zeppelin* carried 24 passengers in luxury. The passenger-carrying gondola included bedrooms, a bathroom, a dining room and an observation deck. There was even a light-weight piano to provide music.

1898 Alberto Santos-Dumont used a small motorcycle engine to power his airship. The engine was powerful enough to drive the ship in any direction, even on a windy day. He built a total of 16 airships which were flown around Paris from 1898 to 1907.

1910-1914 Between 1910 and 1914 the Zeppelin company operated the first regular passenger service between Lake Constance, Berlin and other German cities. The Zeppelin airships carried 35,000 passengers before the start of World War One. During the war, they were used for bombing and reconnaissance flights.

1913 A US Navy C-7 non-rigid airship used for sea patrols, seeking enemy ships and submarines. They were ideal for this work because they were capable of long flights in bad weather. During World War One, these airships protected ships from submarine attack.

1926 The Norge airship was the most successful of the large non-rigid airships built after World War One in Italy. It carried a crew of 16, including the Norwegian explorer Roald Amundsen and Italian Umberto Nobile, to the North Pole in 1926. Two years later Nobile crashed a similar airship, the *Italia*, on a second trip to the North Pole. Amundsen was killed attempting to rescue him.

1936 The Zeppelin airship, *Hindenburg*, was launched in 1936. It is still the largest object that has ever flown. It was 245 metres in length, three times the length of a modern jumbo jet. The giant airship could carry 75 passengers and a crew of 25.

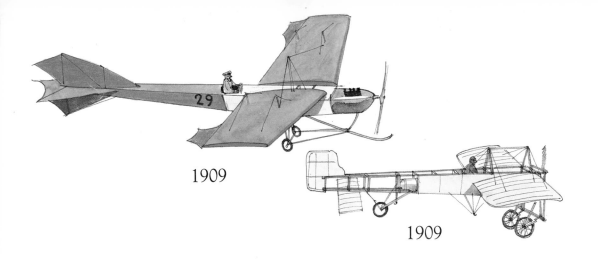

1909

1909

IMPROVING THE AIRPLANE

Developed in 1909, the rotary engine gave aviation pioneers the light-weight power source that they needed.

Spurred on by the success of the Wright brothers in 1903, European aviators soon took to the skies. Alberto Santos-Dumont, the airship builder, was the first to fly in Europe, on 23 October, 1906. Over the next few years there was rapid progress in aircraft design. Unlike the Wright brothers, European designers preferred to have a rear-mounted elevator and a propeller at the front. Also, better and more powerful engines were developed in Europe.

In August 1909, aviators assembled at Rheims in France to hold an air show where they could show off their latest machines and compete against each other. There were 38 machines and 22 pilots. They completed 87 flights of more than 4.8 kilometres. The greatest distance covered in a single flight was 180 kilometres by Frenchman Henri Farman. The highest altitude reached was 152 metres by an Antoinette monoplane. These successes proved that the airplane had developed from a contraption made of sticks and string to a reliable flying machine.

A poster (left) advertising the Rheims air show promises a day of excitement. The highest speed achieved at the show was 76 km/h by Louis Blériot in a Blériot XII (above). American Glenn Curtiss's *Golden Flier* (below) also flew well, reaching a speed of 69 km/h. A Wright biplane (right) was flown by Eugene Lefebvre, but it could not match the speed of Blériot or Curtiss.

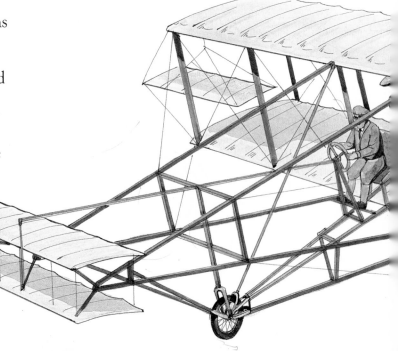

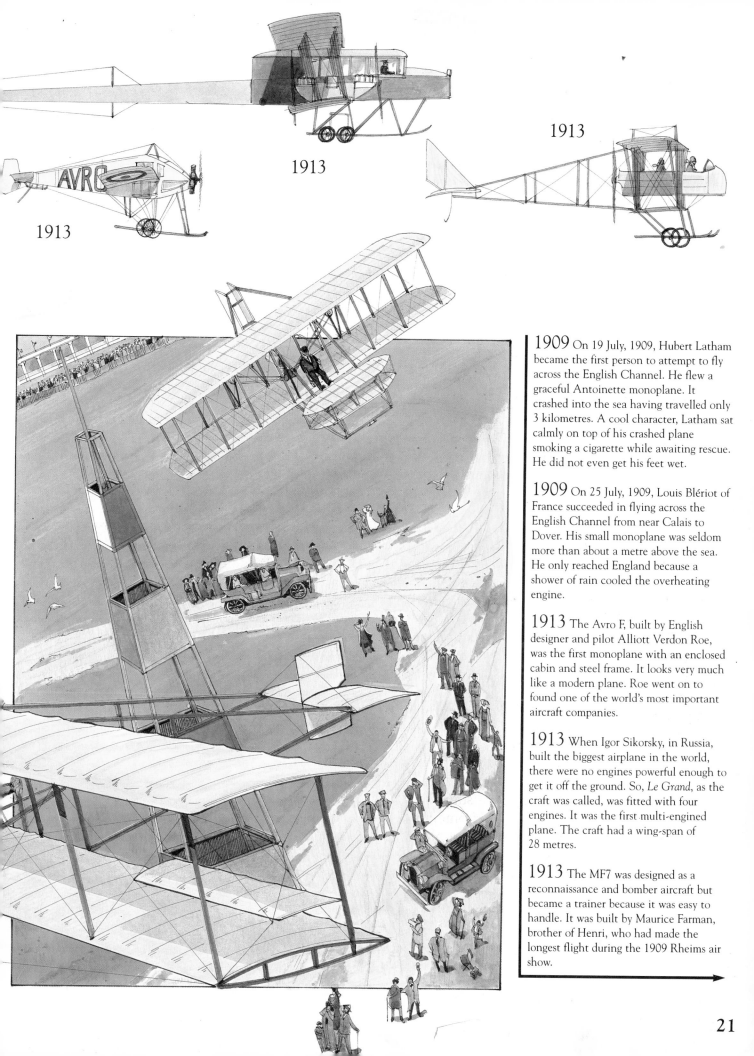

1913

1913

1913

1913

1909 On 19 July, 1909, Hubert Latham became the first person to attempt to fly across the English Channel. He flew a graceful Antoinette monoplane. It crashed into the sea having travelled only 3 kilometres. A cool character, Latham sat calmly on top of his crashed plane smoking a cigarette while awaiting rescue. He did not even get his feet wet.

1909 On 25 July, 1909, Louis Blériot of France succeeded in flying across the English Channel from near Calais to Dover. His small monoplane was seldom more than about a metre above the sea. He only reached England because a shower of rain cooled the overheating engine.

1913 The Avro F, built by English designer and pilot Alliott Verdon Roe, was the first monoplane with an enclosed cabin and steel frame. It looks very much like a modern plane. Roe went on to found one of the world's most important aircraft companies.

1913 When Igor Sikorsky, in Russia, built the biggest airplane in the world, there were no engines powerful enough to get it off the ground. So, *Le Grand*, as the craft was called, was fitted with four engines. It was the first multi-engined plane. The craft had a wing-span of 28 metres.

1913 The MF7 was designed as a reconnaissance and bomber aircraft but became a trainer because it was easy to handle. It was built by Maurice Farman, brother of Henri, who had made the longest flight during the 1909 Rheims air show.

1914

1915

1916

WORLD WAR ONE

Manfred von Richthofen, the German air ace, shot down 80 aircraft before being killed in action.

When World War One began in 1914 the main task for aircraft was to gather information for use by the opposing armies and navies. As the war went on, pilots adopted a more aggressive line. They took rifles and pistols to shoot at the enemy. There were also attempts to drop grenades and boxes of darts onto enemy aircraft, or to stop the enemy's propeller by tangling a length of rope around it. After a time, machine guns were installed and the plane became a fully fledged weapon. The new fighting machines were used by air aces to engage in pitched battles, or dog fights. Germany's Manfred von Richthofen is probably one of the best-known fighter pilots. Britain, too, had its air aces, such as Albert Ball, who shot down at least 42 enemy planes.

The long-range bomber made its appearance during the war. The early attempts at bombing were crude – pilots simply dropped small bombs from their aircraft's cabin. Germany used Zeppelin airships for bombing raids, although they did little damage to their targets. Soon planes that could carry large loads of bombs were developed. The Italian Caproni bomber, and others like it, played a considerable part in the history of World War One.

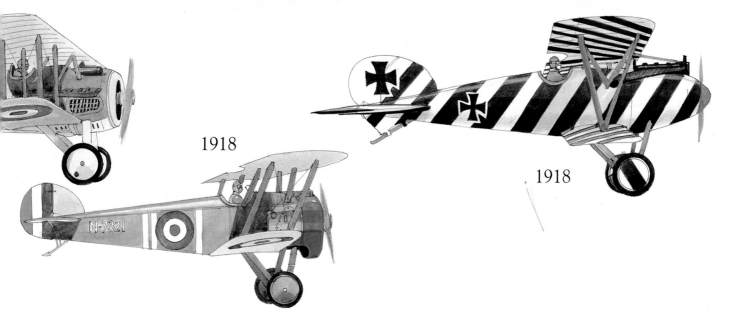

1918

1918

THE ITALIAN Caproni bomber, which entered service in 1915, was among the first large bombers built. It could carry a 450-kilo bomb load and made raids over the Alps from Italy to attack targets in Austria. During the flights, which lasted several hours, the gunners had to stand on open platforms, behind the top wing, in the bitter cold.

1914 The first true fighter plane, the Fokker monoplane. This German aircraft had an 'interrupter' which allowed machine gun bullets to pass between the blades of the turning propeller. This made it easy for the pilot to aim the gun. The Fokker monoplane was one of the most successful planes of the war.

1915 The British B.E. 2c reconnaissance airplane. It was built in large numbers as an all-purpose aircraft and used for reconnaissance and artillery observation. It was a good, steady plane but could not manoeuvre quickly and was outclassed by 1917. Nevertheless, it managed to shoot down some Zeppelin airships.

1916 The SPAD 13, the best French fighter of World War One. It was a highly effective aircraft, even though it only carried a single gun. It was fast and could reach 190 km/h.

1918 The Sopwith Camel, the mainstay of the British fighters in the final years of the war. They were used to strafe (fire at) ground targets and were excellent in aerial dog fights. The Camel destroyed over 3,000 enemy aircraft to become the most successful fighter of World War One. It was the crew of one of these planes that shot down the German ace, Manfred von Richthofen.

1918 The Albatross D Va, a typical German fighter of the last years of World War One. These craft were less agile than some British planes, but were still formidable fighters.

GERMAN ACE PILOT Manfred von Richthofen in a Fokker triplane attacks a British Bristol F.2B over France. Known as the Red Baron because his triplane was mainly painted red, Richthofen was the most successful fighter pilot of World War One. Fighter pilots liked to gain height and dive down on the enemy. Height was important because a pilot could be hidden by clouds or the glare of the sun and dive on the enemy with extra speed.

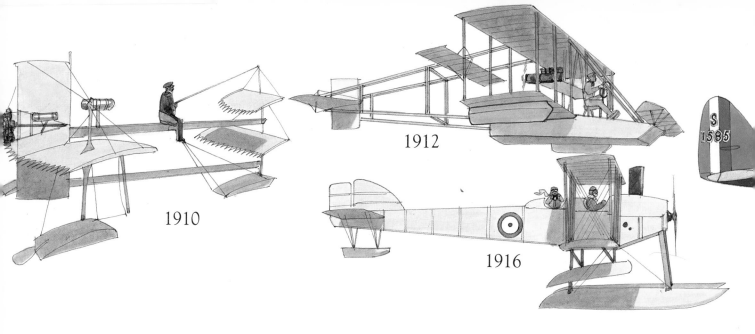

1910

1912

1916

FROM THE SEA

Logo of Pan American Airways. In the 1930s PAA built up a reputation for long-distance travel across the Pacific and Atlantic.

There were few airports in the early days of aviation, so aircraft were built to take off and land on waterways and oceans. The first person to fly an aircraft from water was a Frenchman named Henri Fabre. He fitted floats under his plane instead of wheels. His plane, called a seaplane, flew for the first time at Martigues, France, on 28 March, 1910. By September that year, Fabre had succeeded in making a flight of 3 kilometres.

The great US pioneer of the seaplane was Glenn Curtiss. He designed and built the first really practical seaplane, which made its first flight was on 26 January, 1911. In 1912, Curtiss invented the flying boat by fitting an aircraft with a single wide float, instead of two narrow ones, and putting seats inside the float.

Early seaplanes were used in air races before and after World War One. The races helped develop new, more powerful engines, enabling aircraft to fly at over 640 km/h for the first time. Flying boats, too, benefitted. By the 1930s, they were carrying large loads over long distances.

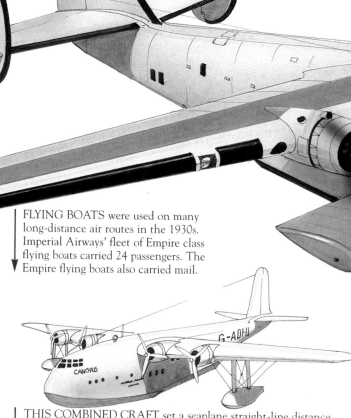

FLYING BOATS were used on many long-distance air routes in the 1930s. Imperial Airways' fleet of Empire class flying boats carried 24 passengers. The Empire flying boats also carried mail.

THIS COMBINED CRAFT set a seaplane straight-line distance record of 9,655 kilometres in 1938. The large flying boat lifted the smaller craft, *Mercury*, into the air, where it was released with a full load of fuel.

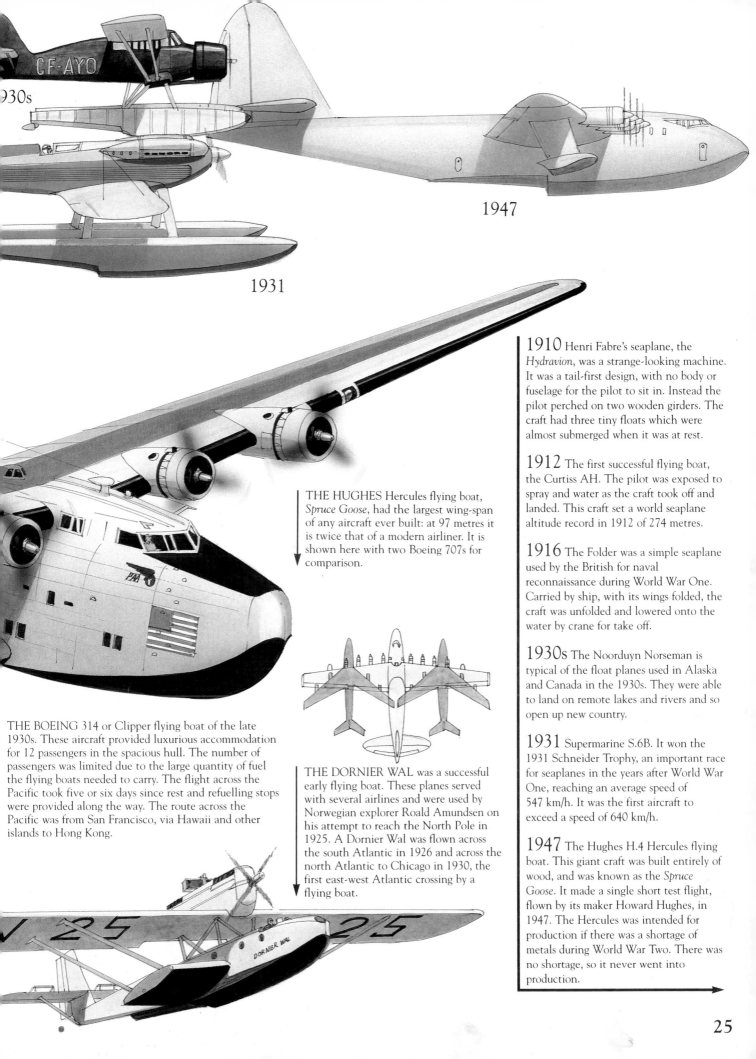

1930s

CF-AYO

1947

1931

THE HUGHES Hercules flying boat, *Spruce Goose*, had the largest wing-span of any aircraft ever built: at 97 metres it is twice that of a modern airliner. It is shown here with two Boeing 707s for comparison.

THE BOEING 314 or Clipper flying boat of the late 1930s. These aircraft provided luxurious accommodation for 12 passengers in the spacious hull. The number of passengers was limited due to the large quantity of fuel the flying boats needed to carry. The flight across the Pacific took five or six days since rest and refuelling stops were provided along the way. The route across the Pacific was from San Francisco, via Hawaii and other islands to Hong Kong.

THE DORNIER WAL was a successful early flying boat. These planes served with several airlines and were used by Norwegian explorer Roald Amundsen on his attempt to reach the North Pole in 1925. A Dornier Wal was flown across the south Atlantic in 1926 and across the north Atlantic to Chicago in 1930, the first east-west Atlantic crossing by a flying boat.

1910 Henri Fabre's seaplane, the *Hydravion*, was a strange-looking machine. It was a tail-first design, with no body or fuselage for the pilot to sit in. Instead the pilot perched on two wooden girders. The craft had three tiny floats which were almost submerged when it was at rest.

1912 The first successful flying boat, the Curtiss AH. The pilot was exposed to spray and water as the craft took off and landed. This craft set a world seaplane altitude record in 1912 of 274 metres.

1916 The Folder was a simple seaplane used by the British for naval reconnaissance during World War One. Carried by ship, with its wings folded, the craft was unfolded and lowered onto the water by crane for take off.

1930s The Noorduyn Norseman is typical of the float planes used in Alaska and Canada in the 1930s. They were able to land on remote lakes and rivers and so open up new country.

1931 Supermarine S.6B. It won the 1931 Schneider Trophy, an important race for seaplanes in the years after World War One, reaching an average speed of 547 km/h. It was the first aircraft to exceed a speed of 640 km/h.

1947 The Hughes H.4 Hercules flying boat. This giant craft was built entirely of wood, and was known as the *Spruce Goose*. It made a single short test flight, flown by its maker Howard Hughes, in 1947. The Hercules was intended for production if there was a shortage of metals during World War Two. There was no shortage, so it never went into production.

25

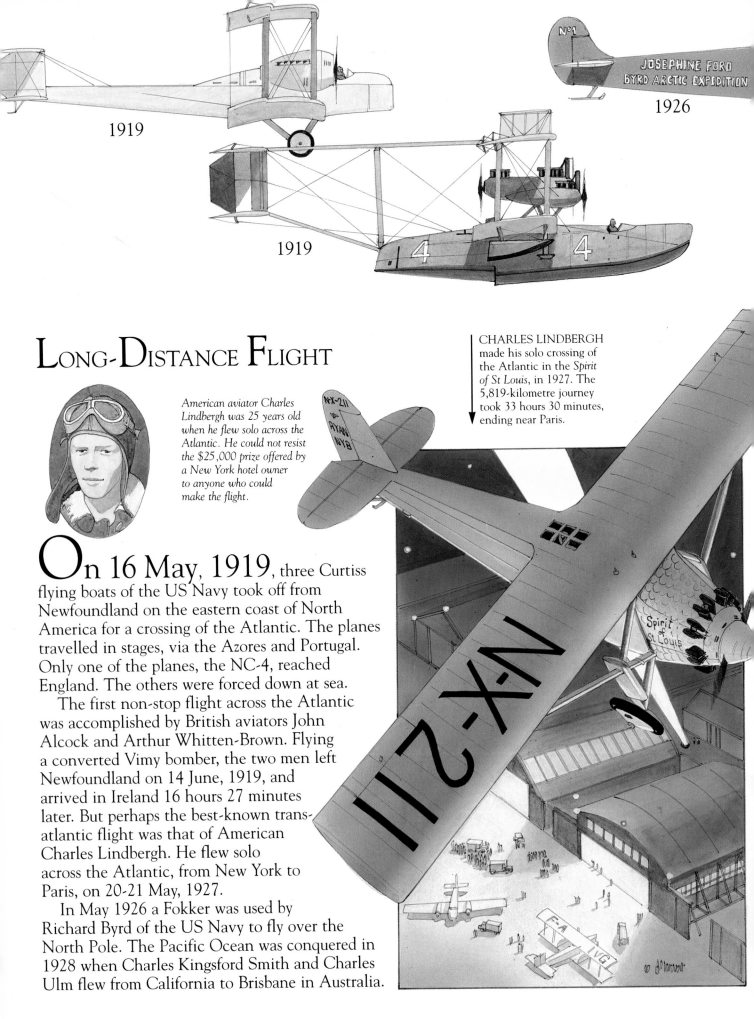

1919

1926

1919

Long-Distance Flight

American aviator Charles Lindbergh was 25 years old when he flew solo across the Atlantic. He could not resist the $25,000 prize offered by a New York hotel owner to anyone who could make the flight.

CHARLES LINDBERGH made his solo crossing of the Atlantic in the *Spirit of St Louis*, in 1927. The 5,819-kilometre journey took 33 hours 30 minutes, ending near Paris.

On 16 May, 1919, three Curtiss flying boats of the US Navy took off from Newfoundland on the eastern coast of North America for a crossing of the Atlantic. The planes travelled in stages, via the Azores and Portugal. Only one of the planes, the NC-4, reached England. The others were forced down at sea.

The first non-stop flight across the Atlantic was accomplished by British aviators John Alcock and Arthur Whitten-Brown. Flying a converted Vimy bomber, the two men left Newfoundland on 14 June, 1919, and arrived in Ireland 16 hours 27 minutes later. But perhaps the best-known trans-atlantic flight was that of American Charles Lindbergh. He flew solo across the Atlantic, from New York to Paris, on 20-21 May, 1927.

In May 1926 a Fokker was used by Richard Byrd of the US Navy to fly over the North Pole. The Pacific Ocean was conquered in 1928 when Charles Kingsford Smith and Charles Ulm flew from California to Brisbane in Australia.

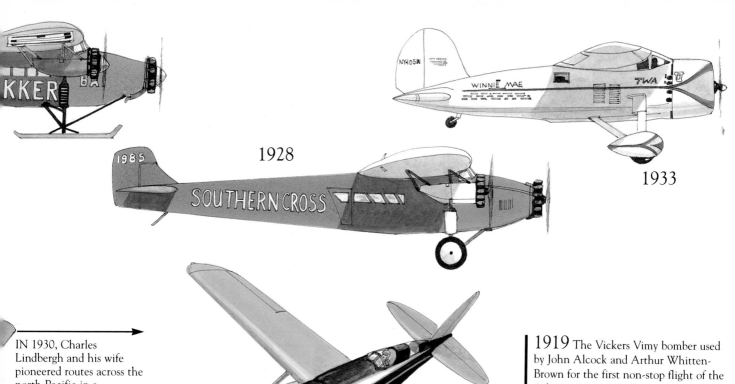

1928

1933

IN 1930, Charles Lindbergh and his wife pioneered routes across the north Pacific in a Lockheed Sirius. They flew to Japan via Alaska, Siberia and the Kurile Islands. The north Pacific had been opened up in 1927, when Americans, Albert Hegenburger and Lester Maitland, flew from California to Hawaii.

IN 1930, English aviator Amy Johnson (left) flew solo from England to Australia in a de Havilland Moth (below). The journey took 9½ days. During the flight she established a record time from London to India of six days. In 1932, she made the fastest ever solo flight from England to Cape Town, South Africa. Her plane vanished mysteriously while flying over the English Channel in 1941.

1919 The Vickers Vimy bomber used by John Alcock and Arthur Whitten-Brown for the first non-stop flight of the Atlantic Ocean. The plane covered the 3,024 kilometres between Newfoundland and Ireland in 16 hours 27 minutes. Other Vimys made the first flights from England to Australia and South Africa.

1919 The Curtiss NC-4 flying boat which completed the first flight across the Atlantic in 1919. During the flight, 68 naval ships took up positions across the ocean, one every 80 kilometres, to guide the aviators. The flight took 54 hours with several refuelling stops.

1926 The Fokker plane used by American explorer Richard Byrd when he flew to the North Pole in 1926. Byrd also flew over the South Pole in 1929. There were 10 aircraft with various expeditions in Antarctica in the summer of 1929. The plane had become an essential tool for the explorer.

1928 *Southern Cross*, the Fokker plane used by Charles Kingsford Smith on the first crossing of the Pacific Ocean. He flew from Oakland, California, to Honolulu, Fiji and then to Brisbane, Australia. The flight took 83 hours flying time. The *Southern Cross* was also used by Kingsford Smith to fly the Tasman Sea between Australia and New Zealand in 1928.

1933 A Lockheed Vega, *Winnie May*, was used by American, Wiley Post, for the first solo round-the-world flight in July 1933. Post covered 24,954 kilometres in 7 days, 18 hours and 49 minutes.

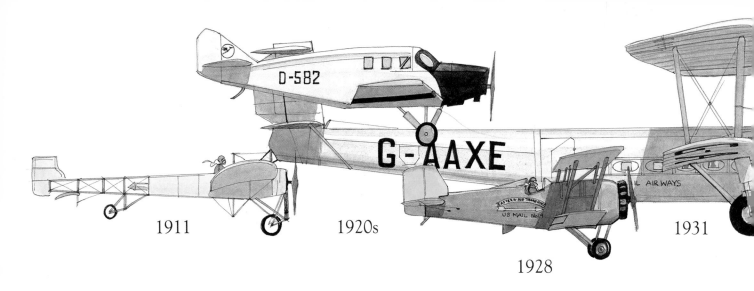

1911   1920s

1928

1931

Putting Airplanes to Work

The German national airline, Lufthansa, was created in 1926. It operated a network of air routes from Berlin.

In 1918, at the end of World War One, there were thousands of planes left over from the war, and many experienced pilots keen to earn a living by flying them. The airplane was soon set to work carrying mail and passengers.

In the USA, nationwide airmail services started in 1918 with war-surplus bombers. It was dangerous work for the pilots: 30 of the first 40 pilots died flying the mail.

The year 1919 saw the real beginnings of the airlines. In February 1919 a German firm started a daily passenger service between Berlin and Weimar. Each plane only carried two passengers, and the flight could not have been comfortable: the passengers sat in the open cockpits of a converted bomber. In August 1919 the first daily international airline service began: between London and Paris using the de Havilland DH9. Passengers were supplied with leather jackets, goggles and flying helmets. They were even given hot water-bottles to help them keep warm during the 2½ hour flight.

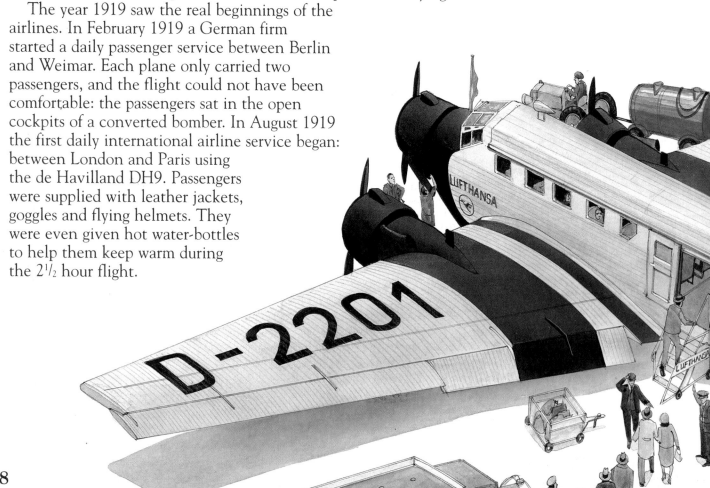

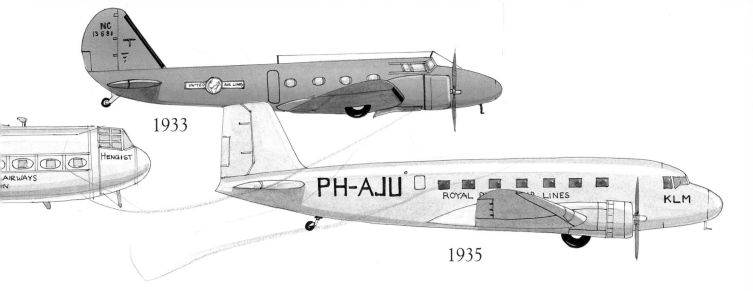

1933

1935

INSIDE THE CABIN of a Silver Wing Argosy of the British Imperial Airways in 1927. The Argosy was a great improvement on earlier airliners. Although the pilots still sat out front in the open, the passengers enjoyed a comfortable cabin.

THE GERMAN JUNKERS F13 was the first purpose-built airliner. It entered service in June 1919. It was an all-metal construction and had an enclosed cabin for the passengers. The Junkers F13 was such a reliable aircraft that the very first F13 built was still flying 20 years later.

IN 1930, Ellen Church and seven other young women became the world's first airline steward-esses. They served passengers on the San Francisco to Chicago service of United Airlines.

1911 To celebrate the coronation of King George V, an airmail service was set up to deliver letters from London to Windsor Castle, 30 kilometres away. The Blériot XI plane used for the service carried about 100,000 letters and postcards during ten days in September, 1911.

1920s The Junkers F13 was the first all-metal airplane designed and built to carry cargo and passengers. More than 300 F13s were built for a wide range of transport duties.

1928 The Pitcairn Super Mailwing was an early airmail carrier. It was used by many mail-carrying airlines in the USA.

1931 The Handley Page 42 was one of the last great biplane airliners. The 42 carried more passengers between London and Europe in the 1930s than all other airliners combined.

1933 The Boeing 247 revolutionized airliner design in 1933. It was fast but, more important, it was one of the first planes that could fly safely if one engine failed. The 247 could fly coast to coast across the USA in 20 hours, three hours faster than its rivals.

1935 The Douglas DC-3, also known as the Dakota, is the most popular airliner of all time. It first flew in 1935 and immediately reduced the journey time across the USA by two hours. Almost every airline in the world has used the DC-3 at one time or another. Thirty years after it was introduced, it still outnumbered any other type of airliner. Many hundreds are still flying today in every corner of the world.

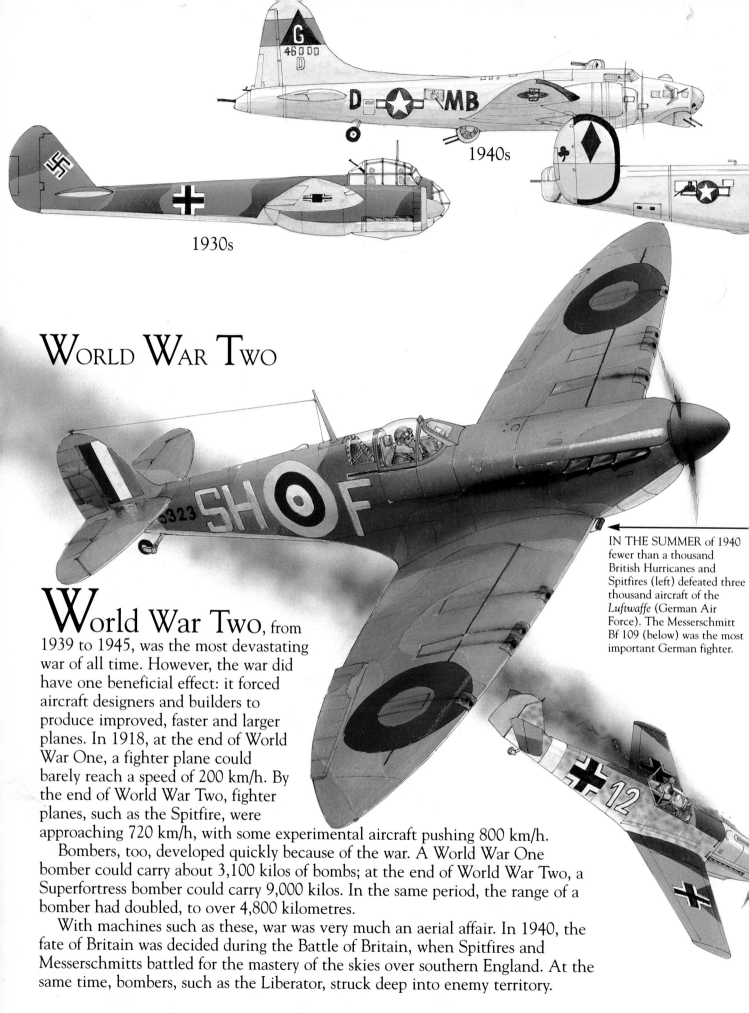

1940s

1930s

WORLD WAR TWO

World War Two, from 1939 to 1945, was the most devastating war of all time. However, the war did have one beneficial effect: it forced aircraft designers and builders to produce improved, faster and larger planes. In 1918, at the end of World War One, a fighter plane could barely reach a speed of 200 km/h. By the end of World War Two, fighter planes, such as the Spitfire, were approaching 720 km/h, with some experimental aircraft pushing 800 km/h.

Bombers, too, developed quickly because of the war. A World War One bomber could carry about 3,100 kilos of bombs; at the end of World War Two, a Superfortress bomber could carry 9,000 kilos. In the same period, the range of a bomber had doubled, to over 4,800 kilometres.

With machines such as these, war was very much an aerial affair. In 1940, the fate of Britain was decided during the Battle of Britain, when Spitfires and Messerschmitts battled for the mastery of the skies over southern England. At the same time, bombers, such as the Liberator, struck deep into enemy territory.

IN THE SUMMER of 1940 fewer than a thousand British Hurricanes and Spitfires (left) defeated three thousand aircraft of the *Luftwaffe* (German Air Force). The Messerschmitt Bf 109 (below) was the most important German fighter.

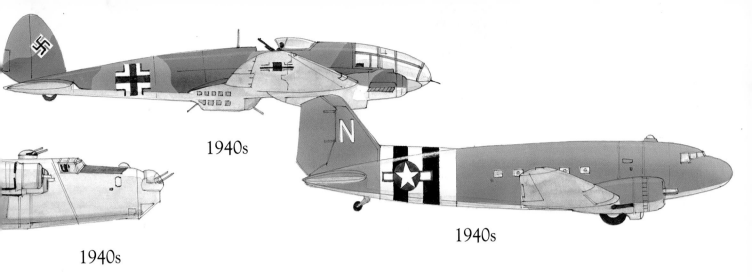

1940s

1940s

1940s

1930s Junkers Ju88. This German aircraft began life as a bomber, but it was tremendously versatile and was also used as a fighter, ground attack and reconnaissance aircraft. It was even used as a guided missile; a small fighter plane was fitted to the top of a pilotless Ju88. The fighter guided the Ju88 to the target and then headed back to base.

1940s B-17 Flying Fortress. This American plane was one of the first giant or heavy bombers. It could fly at a high altitude, carry a large bomb load and had a long range. It was used to destroy factories and communications by accurate bombing from great height. It was fitted with up to 30 guns and attacking it took considerable courage.

THE JAPANESE AICHI D3A dive-bomber which attacked the American forces at Pearl Harbor in December 1941, bringing the USA into the war.

THE LOCKHEED P-38 LIGHTNING (left) was known to the Japanese as the 'Fork-tailed Devil'. It was responsible for destroying more enemy aircraft in the Pacific than any other fighter. The Mitsubishi A6M (below), known as the 'Zero', was Japan's most important fighter of World War Two. It flew from shore bases and aircraft carriers in the Pacific. It was fast, highly manoeuvrable and could quickly reach an altitude of around 4,700 metres.

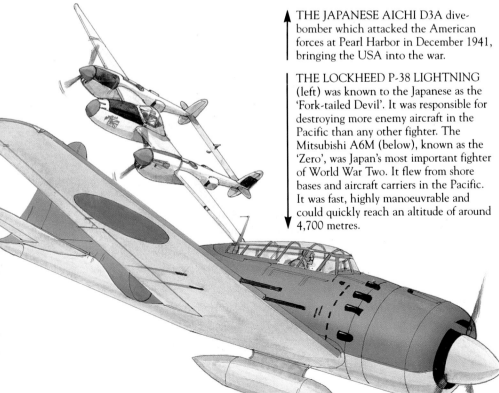

1940s B-24 Liberator. During the war, the heart of Germany was attacked by vast fleets of heavy, four-engined bombers, such as the American B-17 Flying Fortress and the B-24 Liberator. The Liberator was also used as a transport and reconnaissance plane. It played a vital part in the Pacific war, too, where its long range was of particular value.

1940s Germany's most important bomber, the Heinkel He 111. A vast variety of types was built. Some were used for torpedo attacks on shipping and others as airborne launching platforms for the jet-propelled V-1 flying bombs.

1940s Douglas DC-4. This was an important American transport plane, used to carry soldiers, supplies and equipment, to drop paratroops and to carry casualties to hospital. After the war, the DC-4 was developed into an airliner.

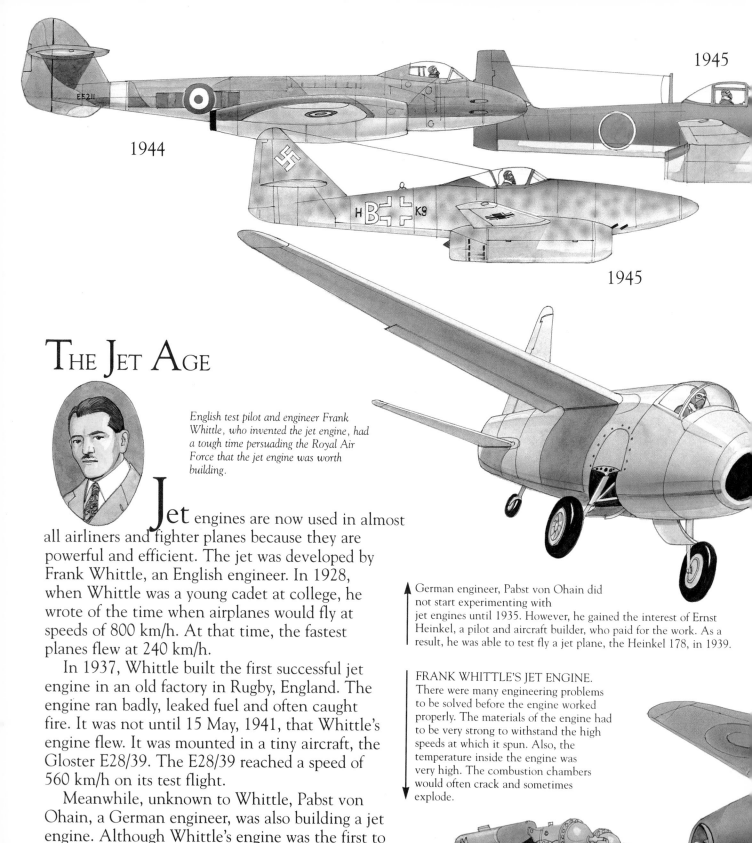

1945

1944

1945

THE JET AGE

English test pilot and engineer Frank Whittle, who invented the jet engine, had a tough time persuading the Royal Air Force that the jet engine was worth building.

Jet engines are now used in almost all airliners and fighter planes because they are powerful and efficient. The jet was developed by Frank Whittle, an English engineer. In 1928, when Whittle was a young cadet at college, he wrote of the time when airplanes would fly at speeds of 800 km/h. At that time, the fastest planes flew at 240 km/h.

In 1937, Whittle built the first successful jet engine in an old factory in Rugby, England. The engine ran badly, leaked fuel and often caught fire. It was not until 15 May, 1941, that Whittle's engine flew. It was mounted in a tiny aircraft, the Gloster E28/39. The E28/39 reached a speed of 560 km/h on its test flight.

Meanwhile, unknown to Whittle, Pabst von Ohain, a German engineer, was also building a jet engine. Although Whittle's engine was the first to run, von Ohain's engine was the first into the air. On 27 August, 1939, the engine was used to power a Heinkel 178 aircraft. However, the Heinkel 178, an experimental prototype, never flew again and today Whittle is remembered as the 'Father of the Jet Engine'.

German engineer, Pabst von Ohain did not start experimenting with jet engines until 1935. However, he gained the interest of Ernst Heinkel, a pilot and aircraft builder, who paid for the work. As a result, he was able to test fly a jet plane, the Heinkel 178, in 1939.

FRANK WHITTLE'S JET ENGINE. There were many engineering problems to be solved before the engine worked properly. The materials of the engine had to be very strong to withstand the high speeds at which it spun. Also, the temperature inside the engine was very high. The combustion chambers would often crack and sometimes explode.

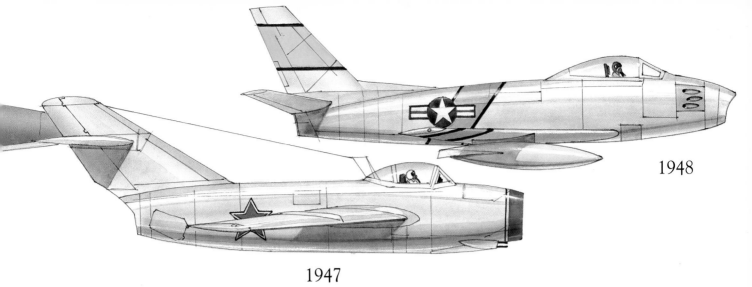

1948

1947

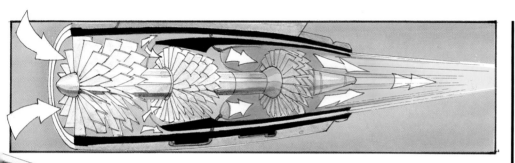

INSIDE A MODERN JET ENGINE. Air is sucked into the engine at the front. Spinning fans compress the air and force it into the combustion chamber. In the combustion chamber, fuel burns in the air. This produces hot gases which expand and rush towards the rear of the engine, giving a forward thrust. The gases turn a turbine which spins the fan at the front. This type of jet engine is called a turbofan engine.

THE FIRST AIRCRAFT to fly with a Whittle jet engine, the Gloster E28/39, took to the air in 1941. Two E28/39s were built and flown for four years. By this time, confidence was high and the Meteor, a twin-jet fighter, was being built to take advantage of the new engine. In the summer of 1944 the Meteor was the first jet-powered fighter to enter service.

1944 The British Gloster Meteor was the first jet fighter to be used in action. On 4 August, 1944, the pilot of a Meteor managed to bring down a V-1 flying bomb by flying alongside and tipping it over with his plane's wingtip.

1945 The German Messerschmitt Me 262 was the second jet fighter to enter service, just a few days after the Gloster Meteor. In March 1945, the 262 took part in an all-jet attack on the Ludendorf bridge over the River Rhine, strafing the gun emplacements. The first jet bomber, the Arado Ar 234, also took part in the attack.

1945 The Nakajima Kikka, Japan's first jet fighter, was built towards the end of World War Two, after the Japanese received sketchy details of the German Me 262. The design and construction of the Nakajima Kikka was completed in a remarkably short time, but the plane came too late to influence the war.

1947 First flown in 1947, the US Sabre jet was the most successful fighter plane in the Korean war (1950-1953). Sabres consistently outfought the USSR's Mig-15s, although this was probably due to the better training of the US pilots. In 1948, the Sabre had set a new world speed record of 1,047 km/h.

1948 The Mikoyan-Gurevich Mig-15 was the USSR's first effective jet fighter. It was the main rival to the US Sabre jet over the skies of Korea in the early 1950s. Although slower, the Mig-15 could climb faster and turn more quickly.

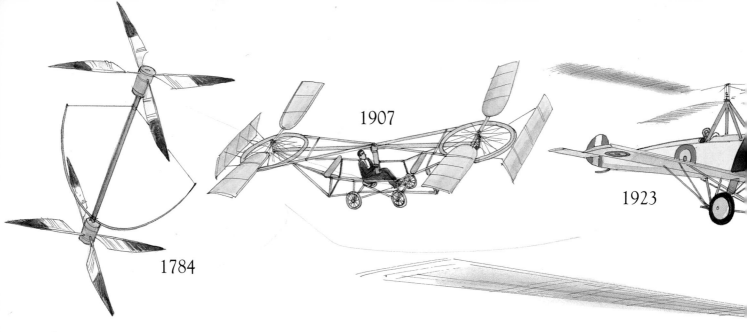

1907

1923

1784

Straight Up and Down

Around 1500, Italian painter and scientist Leonardo da Vinci designed a helicopter. It consisted of a corkscrew-shaped blade which he thought would rise upwards as it spun.

The idea behind the helicopter is an old one. Around 2,500 years ago, the Chinese built spinning tops which rose into the air as they spun. It proved difficult, however, to turn the toy into a full-sized flying machine. The first helicopter to get off the ground carrying a person was a French contraption called the Bregeut-Richet No 1. On 29 September, 1907, it struggled into the air, held firmly by four people on the ground for safety. It only rose 0.6 metre and stayed in the air for just over 60 seconds. Two months later, Paul Cornu at Lisieux, France, made the first untethered helicopter flight. His machine rose only 30 centimetres and stayed up for 20 seconds before crashing.

There were two problems facing helicopter designers. The first was to stop the helicopter spinning in the opposite direction to the rotors (spinning blades). The other was to stop the helicopter tipping over as it rose. Both problems were solved in the 1930s. In 1935 a French machine, the Bregeut-Dorand, climbed to 155 metres and flew for over an hour. Then, in 1939, Igor Sikorsky, a Russian exile living in America, built the first modern-style helicopter, with a small rear rotor.

IGOR SIKORSKY made the first flight in his VS-300 helicopter on 14 September, 1939. By this time most of the problems of controlling a helicopter had been solved. The main rotor blades were able to twist as they turned, enabling them to produce a steady lifting force. This ensured that the helicopter did not tip over as it rose. The rotor could also be tilted to allow the helicopter to move forward or backward. Sikorsky added another refinement, a small rear rotor to stop the machine spinning in flight.

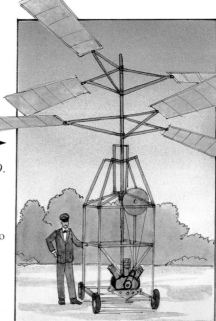

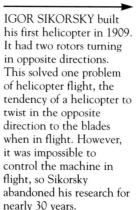

IGOR SIKORSKY built his first helicopter in 1909. It had two rotors turning in opposite directions. This solved one problem of helicopter flight, the tendency of a helicopter to twist in the opposite direction to the blades when in flight. However, it was impossible to control the machine in flight, so Sikorsky abandoned his research for nearly 30 years.

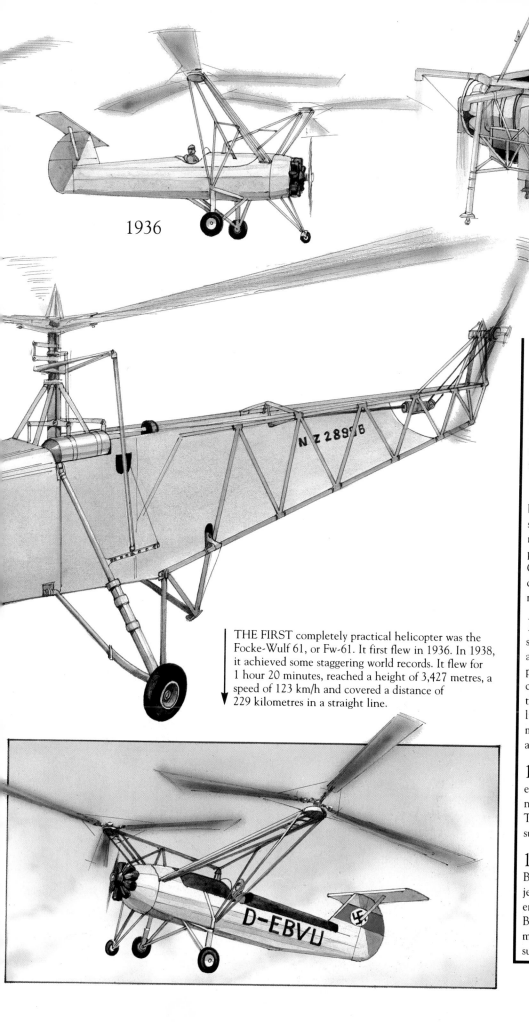

1936

1954

N Z 2895 B

THE FIRST completely practical helicopter was the Focke-Wulf 61, or Fw-61. It first flew in 1936. In 1938, it achieved some staggering world records. It flew for 1 hour 20 minutes, reached a height of 3,427 metres, a speed of 123 km/h and covered a distance of 229 kilometres in a straight line.

D-EBVU

1784 A model helicopter made in France in 1784. It had two propellers, one at each end, which were turned in opposite directions by pulling on a wound string. Because the propellers turned in opposite directions, the toy did not twist in flight. This method of preventing unwanted spin was not to be rediscovered for another 150 years.

1907 The twin-rotor helicopter made by Frenchman Paul Cornu. It made a short, untethered flight in 1907. The rotors spun in opposite directions like the propellers of the French toy of 1784. Cornu did not have the money to continue his experiments and helicopter research came to a halt for many years.

1923 Spaniard Juan de la Cierva built a strange-looking machine, called an autogyro, in 1923. It was an ordinary plane with a rotor fitted above the cockpit. The rotor blades were turned by the airflow as the craft moved forward, like the sails of a windmill, and lifted the machine. In 1928 Cierva flew an autogyro across the English Channel.

1936 The Focke-Achgelis Fa-61 was an early German helicopter, though it was not really practical. It first flew in 1936. The basic design was developed into the successful Fw-61.

1954 The vertical take-off 'Flying Bedstead' became the first vertical take-off jet in 1954. It achieved its lift by using jet engines pointing downwards. The 'Flying Bedstead' is the direct ancestor of the modern vertical take-off fighter planes, such as the British Harrier 'jump jet'.

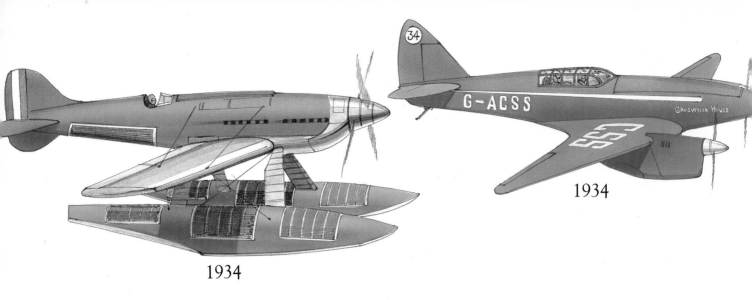

1934

1934

FASTER AND FASTER

The Gee Bee Super Sportster, one of the smallest airplanes, set a speed record of 470 km/h in 1932. It was almost all engine!

When Orville Wright first flew in 1903, he reached a speed of only 11 km/h. Then, in 1909, the Frenchman Louis Blériot reached a speed of 76 km/h at the Rheims air show. From these modest beginnings, aircraft speeds have increased steadily.

An important milestone in flying history occurred on 14 October, 1947, when Captain Chuck Yeager of the US Air Force flew a rocket plane, called *Glamorous Glennis* after his wife, faster than the speed of sound (about 1,220 km/h at sea level). Many people had thought that it was impossible to fly faster than sound – they talked of a 'sound barrier' which could not be broken. Today the world air-speed record, held by the X-15, another rocket-powered plane, has reached 7,247 km/h, over six times the speed of sound.

The fastest jet plane, the Lockheed SR-71 or Blackbird, reached a speed of 3,529 km/h, over three times the speed of sound, in 1976. The SR-71 was used for spy flights over enemy territory. The fastest combat jet is the Russian Mikoyan Mig-25, which has reached a speed of 3,395 km/h.

THE LOCKHEED SR-71 or Blackbird. The thin skin of the Blackbird was painted with a special black paint which could withstand high temperatures. The skin reached a temperature of over 300°C during flight.

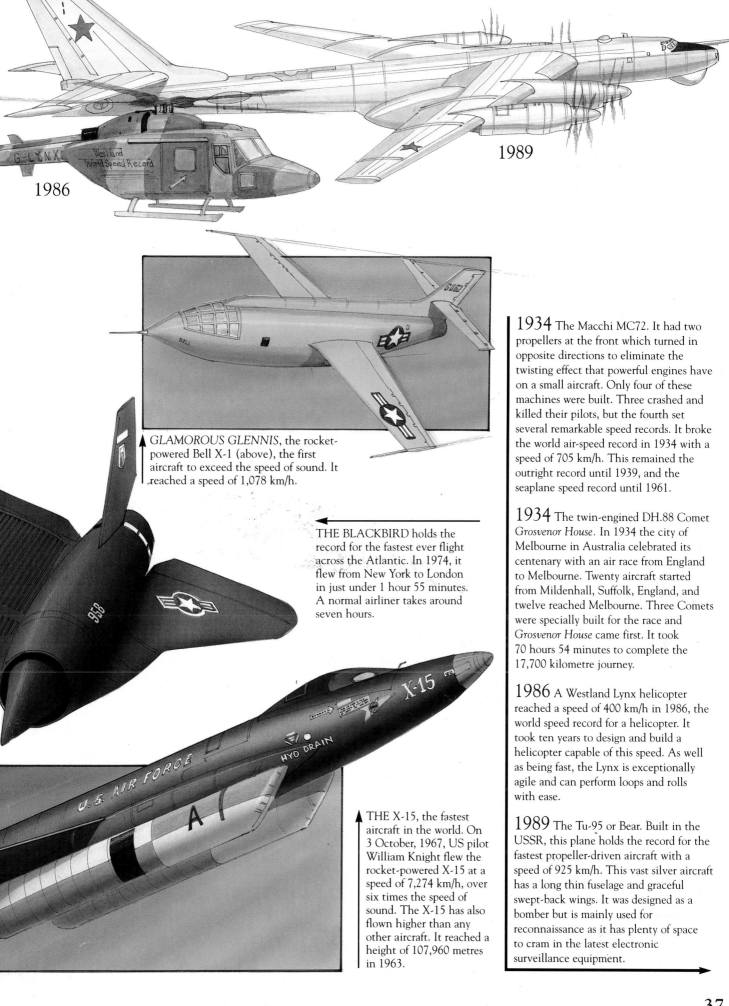

1989

1986

GLAMOROUS GLENNIS, the rocket-powered Bell X-1 (above), the first aircraft to exceed the speed of sound. It reached a speed of 1,078 km/h.

THE BLACKBIRD holds the record for the fastest ever flight across the Atlantic. In 1974, it flew from New York to London in just under 1 hour 55 minutes. A normal airliner takes around seven hours.

THE X-15, the fastest aircraft in the world. On 3 October, 1967, US pilot William Knight flew the rocket-powered X-15 at a speed of 7,274 km/h, over six times the speed of sound. The X-15 has also flown higher than any other aircraft. It reached a height of 107,960 metres in 1963.

1934 The Macchi MC72. It had two propellers at the front which turned in opposite directions to eliminate the twisting effect that powerful engines have on a small aircraft. Only four of these machines were built. Three crashed and killed their pilots, but the fourth set several remarkable speed records. It broke the world air-speed record in 1934 with a speed of 705 km/h. This remained the outright record until 1939, and the seaplane speed record until 1961.

1934 The twin-engined DH.88 Comet *Grosvenor House*. In 1934 the city of Melbourne in Australia celebrated its centenary with an air race from England to Melbourne. Twenty aircraft started from Mildenhall, Suffolk, England, and twelve reached Melbourne. Three Comets were specially built for the race and *Grosvenor House* came first. It took 70 hours 54 minutes to complete the 17,700 kilometre journey.

1986 A Westland Lynx helicopter reached a speed of 400 km/h in 1986, the world speed record for a helicopter. It took ten years to design and build a helicopter capable of this speed. As well as being fast, the Lynx is exceptionally agile and can perform loops and rolls with ease.

1989 The Tu-95 or Bear. Built in the USSR, this plane holds the record for the fastest propeller-driven aircraft with a speed of 925 km/h. This vast silver aircraft has a long thin fuselage and graceful swept-back wings. It was designed as a bomber but is mainly used for reconnaissance as it has plenty of space to cram in the latest electronic surveillance equipment.

37

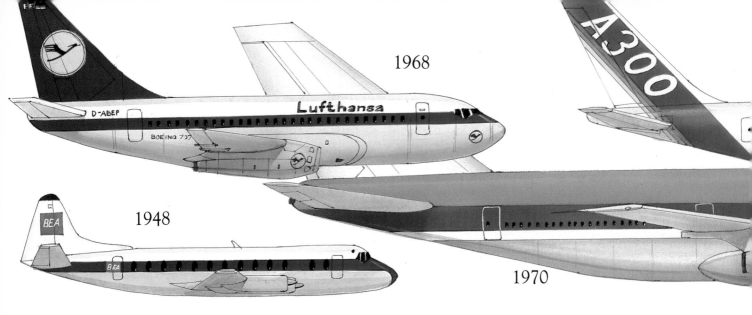

1968

1948

1970

At The Airport

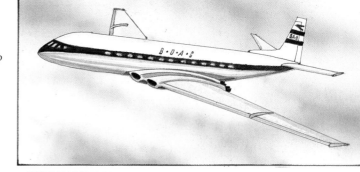

The de Havilland Comet carried fare-paying passengers for the first time in 1952, on a trip to South Africa. Two years later the plane was grounded after two crashes.

A busy airport is an exciting place, with planes taking off and landing. Many different types of plane can be seen from the viewing lounge of the terminal.

Most modern airliners are powered by jet engines. The first jet airliner was the de Havilland Comet which flew for the first time in 1949. The Comet could cruise at 784 km/h at heights well above most of the bad weather, and set new standards in passenger comfort. Another early jet airliner was the Vickers Viscount which began operating in 1953. The first of the really big jets was the Boeing 707. It entered service in 1958 and was soon used on air routes throughout the world. The jumbo jet, or Boeing 747, entered service in 1969.

THERE HAVE BEEN SEVERAL versions of the Boeing 747 or jumbo jet. The 747-400 (below) is distinguished by the vertical winglet at the end of each wing to reduce drag. The Boeing 767 (bottom right) carries 267 passengers on long-distance flights.

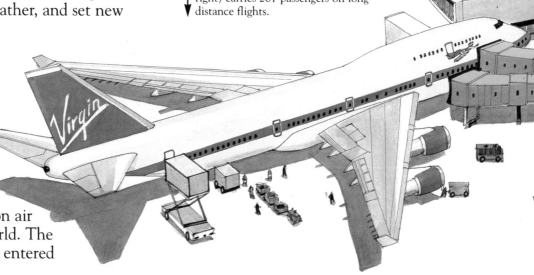

Supersonic (faster-than-sound) passenger services arrived on 1 January, 1968. The Russian Tu-144 took off with 140 passengers and reached a speed of 2,288 km/h, more than twice the speed of sound. The Anglo-French Concorde, now the only supersonic airliner operating, entered service in 1977. It carries passengers across the Atlantic at a speed of 2,166 km/h, making a journey time of three hours.

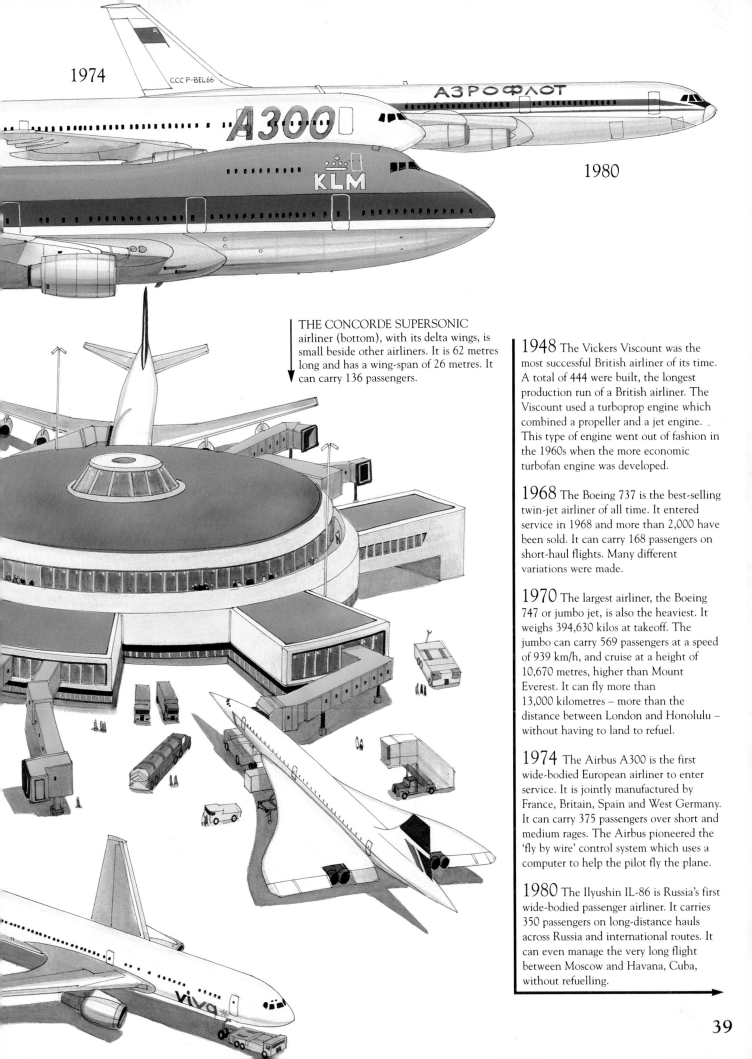

1974

CCC P-BEL66

A300

KLM

АЭРОФЛОТ

1980

THE CONCORDE SUPERSONIC airliner (bottom), with its delta wings, is small beside other airliners. It is 62 metres long and has a wing-span of 26 metres. It can carry 136 passengers.

viva

1948 The Vickers Viscount was the most successful British airliner of its time. A total of 444 were built, the longest production run of a British airliner. The Viscount used a turboprop engine which combined a propeller and a jet engine. This type of engine went out of fashion in the 1960s when the more economic turbofan engine was developed.

1968 The Boeing 737 is the best-selling twin-jet airliner of all time. It entered service in 1968 and more than 2,000 have been sold. It can carry 168 passengers on short-haul flights. Many different variations were made.

1970 The largest airliner, the Boeing 747 or jumbo jet, is also the heaviest. It weighs 394,630 kilos at takeoff. The jumbo can carry 569 passengers at a speed of 939 km/h, and cruise at a height of 10,670 metres, higher than Mount Everest. It can fly more than 13,000 kilometres – more than the distance between London and Honolulu – without having to land to refuel.

1974 The Airbus A300 is the first wide-bodied European airliner to enter service. It is jointly manufactured by France, Britain, Spain and West Germany. It can carry 375 passengers over short and medium rages. The Airbus pioneered the 'fly by wire' control system which uses a computer to help the pilot fly the plane.

1980 The Ilyushin IL-86 is Russia's first wide-bodied passenger airliner. It carries 350 passengers on long-distance hauls across Russia and international routes. It can even manage the very long flight between Moscow and Havana, Cuba, without refuelling.

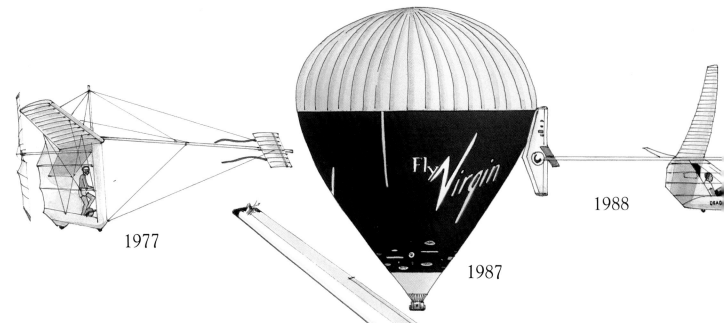

1977

Fly Virgin

1988

1987

Modern Record Breakers

US cyclist Bryan Allen, pilot of Gossamer Albatross, *the first human-powered aircraft to cross the English Channel.*

In recent years, there have been many great aviation achievements. One was the achievement of an age-old dream: the flight of the first human-powered plane, the *Gossamer Condor*, in 1977. Then, in 1979, a human-powered plane, the *Gossamer Albatross*, flew across the English Channel.

Solar-powered aircraft have been flown for the first time, too. A solar-powered plane, the *Solar Challenger*, flew across the English Channel in 1981. The 262-kilometre flight from Paris to Kent took over 5 hours. In 1995 the first solar-powered, pilotless aircraft, *Pathfinder* flew. It can fly for days at a time surveying the ground below.

Another great achievement was the first non-stop, round the world flight without refuelling. The flight started on 14 December, 1986, when Americans Dick Rutan and Jeana Yeager flew *Voyager*, a specially built aircraft, from Edwards Air Force Base, California. Just over nine days later they arrived back at the base, having been aloft ever since leaving.

Balloonists have pressed their craft to the limits, too. American pilot Joe Kittinger made the first solo transatlantic crossing in a helium-filled balloon in 1984.

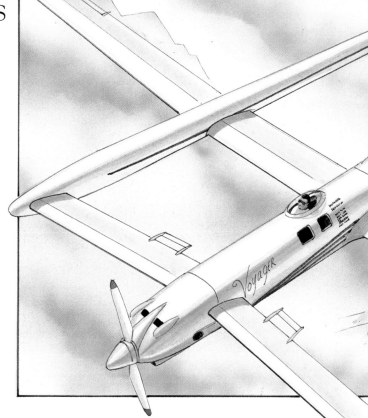

▲ VOYAGER ON THE FIRST ROUND-THE-WORLD flight without refuelling. The plane, with a wing-span of 34 metres, was really a large flying fuel tank. It carried nearly five times its own weight in fuel.

▼ PATHFINDER IS A SOLAR-POWERED flying wing, 30 metres across with eight propellers. Although it first flew in 1995, it is still in the experimental stage.

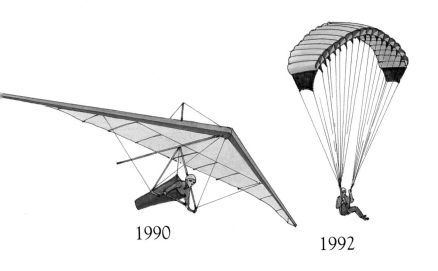

1990

1992

1994

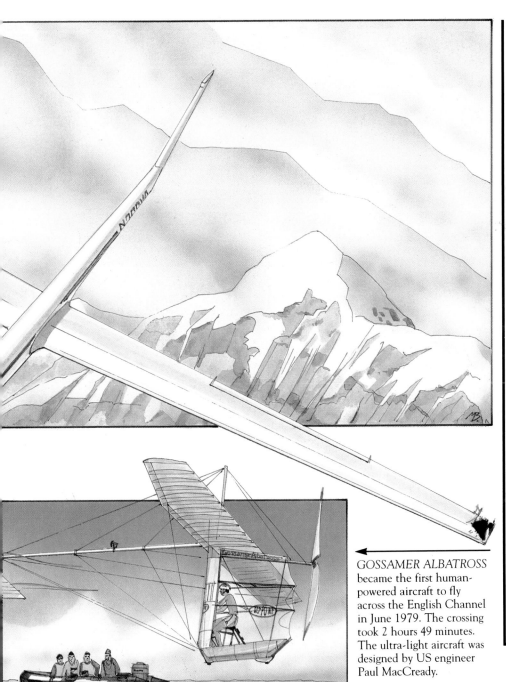

GOSSAMER ALBATROSS became the first human-powered aircraft to fly across the English Channel in June 1979. The crossing took 2 hours 49 minutes. The ultra-light aircraft was designed by US engineer Paul MacCready.

1977 The *Gossamer Condor* made an ancient dream come true. On 23 August 1977 Bryan Allen flew the plane for 7 minutes 27½ seconds. The plane was designed by Paul MacCready and weighed 37.75 kilos. The pilot weighed 61.2 kilos.

1987 British balloonists Richard Branson and Per Lindstrand were the first to cross the Atlantic in a hot-air, as opposed to a gas-filled, balloon in 1987. They covered the 4,947 kilometres from the USA to Ireland in just under 32 hours.

1988 The Greek cyclist, Kanellos Kanellopoulos, recreated the myth of Daedalus, who escaped from Crete on wings. Kanellopoulos flew from Crete to the island of Santorini, 118 kilometres away, entirely under his own power, in an extra-light flying machine called *Daedalus*. The aircraft reached a speed of 29 km/h and was never more than 5 metres above the sea.

1990 The greatest distance flown by a hang-glider is the 488 kilometres achieved by American Larry Tudor in 1990. He flew from New Mexico to Kansas, USA.

1992 Alex Lowse from South Africa flew 282 kilometres by paraglider (gliding parachute) in 1992. The paraglider height record is 4,470 metres, achieved by Robby Whittal in South Africa in 1993.

1994 The smallest jet ever flown is the *Silver Bullet*. Built by American, Bob Bishop, *Silver Bullet* has a wing-span of only 5.2 metres, but it can reach a speed of 450 km/h.

1982

1984

The main engines are used to slow the Shuttle during re-entry.

THE PRESENT DAY

The mission badge of the Columbia Space Shuttle, first flown in 1981.

The fighter planes of today can fly through the air faster than a rifle bullet, at 2,850 km/h (twice the speed of sound). The US Air Force's F15-E, called the Eagle, can fly at almost three times the speed of sound. This is over 260 times faster than the speed Orville Wright managed during his historic flight. Modern aircraft are not only fast – they can be very large. The largest of all is the Russian Antonov An-255. This has a wing-span of 73 metres, six times the span of the Wright *Flyer*.

So, in just over 90 years, aviation has made remarkable progress. This progress is shown most clearly in the Space Shuttle – a plane than goes into space. The US Space Shuttle is blasted into space by powerful rockets. The Shuttle must reach a speed of about 28,000 km/h to get into orbit around the earth. It is when returning to earth that the Shuttle looks and behaves most like an ordinary plane. It glides down through the atmosphere just as the early gliders did. The lessons learned by the pioneers are still of value today, and will remain so in the future.

The Space Shuttle is the size of a jet airliner, 37 metres long and with a wing-span of 24 metres. The astronauts who pilot the Shuttle ride in the cabin at the front, as in an ordinary aircraft. In the middle of the Shuttle is the cargo bay. The Shuttle can carry 29 tonnes of cargo into orbit and bring satellites back to earth for repair. At the rear are three large rocket engines; during launch these are fed with fuel from a large external tank strapped to the Shuttle. The tank is separated from the Shuttle as it rises into space.

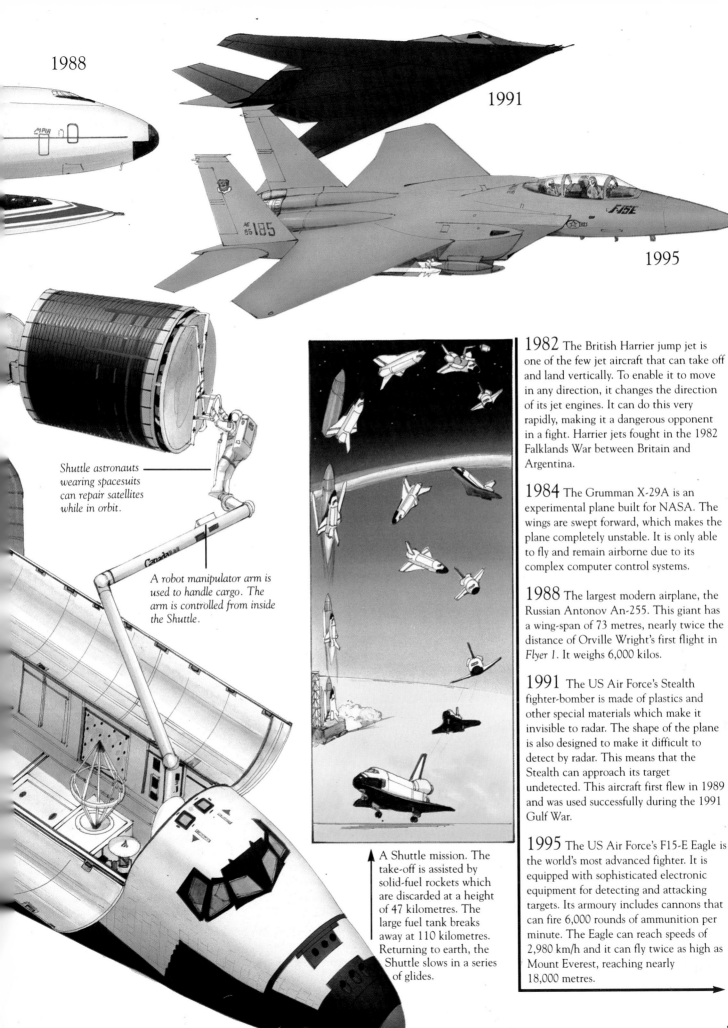

1988

1991

1995

Shuttle astronauts wearing spacesuits can repair satellites while in orbit.

A robot manipulator arm is used to handle cargo. The arm is controlled from inside the Shuttle.

▲ A Shuttle mission. The take-off is assisted by solid-fuel rockets which are discarded at a height of 47 kilometres. The large fuel tank breaks away at 110 kilometres. Returning to earth, the Shuttle slows in a series of glides.

1982 The British Harrier jump jet is one of the few jet aircraft that can take off and land vertically. To enable it to move in any direction, it changes the direction of its jet engines. It can do this very rapidly, making it a dangerous opponent in a fight. Harrier jets fought in the 1982 Falklands War between Britain and Argentina.

1984 The Grumman X-29A is an experimental plane built for NASA. The wings are swept forward, which makes the plane completely unstable. It is only able to fly and remain airborne due to its complex computer control systems.

1988 The largest modern airplane, the Russian Antonov An-255. This giant has a wing-span of 73 metres, nearly twice the distance of Orville Wright's first flight in *Flyer 1*. It weighs 6,000 kilos.

1991 The US Air Force's Stealth fighter-bomber is made of plastics and other special materials which make it invisible to radar. The shape of the plane is also designed to make it difficult to detect by radar. This means that the Stealth can approach its target undetected. This aircraft first flew in 1989 and was used successfully during the 1991 Gulf War.

1995 The US Air Force's F15-E Eagle is the world's most advanced fighter. It is equipped with sophisticated electronic equipment for detecting and attacking targets. Its armoury includes cannons that can fire 6,000 rounds of ammunition per minute. The Eagle can reach speeds of 2,980 km/h and it can fly twice as high as Mount Everest, reaching nearly 18,000 metres.

43

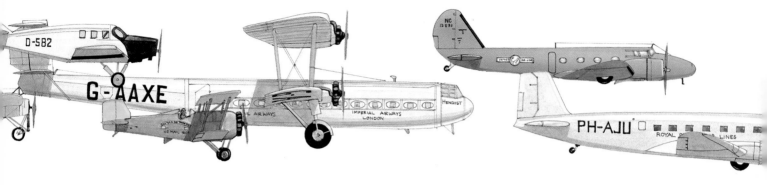

Aviation Facts

The fastest time for a round-the-world flight using regular airline flights is 44 hours 6 minutes. The record was set by Englishman David Springbett in 1980, who travelled 37,124 kilometres from Los Angeles, via London, Bahrain, Singapore, Bangkok, Manila, Tokyo, Honolulu, and back to Los Angeles.

The greatest number of passengers ever carried by an airplane is 1,087 people. A Boeing jumbo jet evacuated this number of people, twice the normal load for a jumbo, from Ethiopia to Israel in 1991.

The largest propeller ever fitted to a plane was 6.9 metres across. It was used on a plane made in Germany in 1919.

A McDonnell Douglas DC-7 airliner has completed over 95,000 flights in 27 years. One jumbo jet has completed over 94,000 hours flying time, and is still going strong.

The longest non-stop regular airline flight is the 12,847-kilometre haul from Johannesburg, South Africa, to New York, USA, flown by South African Airways.

The shortest airline service is by Loganair between the islands of Westray and Papa Westray in the Orkney Islands, north of Scotland. Normally the flight takes two minutes, but with a following wind, it can be over in 58 seconds.

On 18 January, 1911, American pilot Eugene Ely, flying a Curtiss biplane, made the first landing of an airplane on a ship.

The first coast-to-coast flight across the USA was made by Calbraith Rodgers in a Wright biplane between 17 September and 5 November, 1911.

American pilot Amelia Earhart achieved the first solo crossing of the Atlantic by a woman on 21 May, 1932.

The busiest airport in the world is Chicago's O'Hare Field Airport, Illinois, USA. It handles over 64 million passengers and 800,000 aircraft each year, equivalent to one takeoff or landing every 39 seconds. Heathrow Airport, near London, handles more international passengers, over 38 million each year.

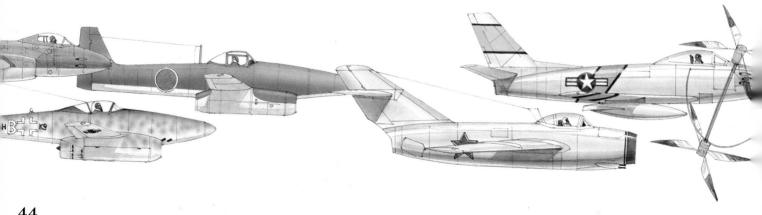

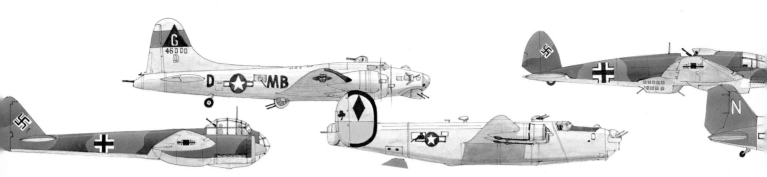

During supersonic flight, Concorde becomes up to 25 centimetres longer; it expands due to the heat generated by supersonic flight. Once when a crew member slotted a book into a gap in the cabin wall of the plane during a flight, he was surprised to find on landing that the gap had disappeared and so had the book. On the next flight, the gap reappeared and the book was recovered.

When a Boeing 747 jumbo jet flies at its cruising speed of 939 km/h, each of its four engines burns about 4.5 litres of fuel every four seconds. At that rate, a family car with a 45-litre tank, would run out of fuel in 10 seconds.

The greatest altitude reached by a passenger-carrying balloon is 37,735 metres. This was achieved by Nicholas Piantanida in South Dakota on 1 February, 1966. Unfortunately, Piantanida crashed and was killed and his flight is not recognized as a record. The official altitude record for a manned balloon is 34,668 metres reached by Malcolm Ross and Victor Prother over the Gulf of Mexico on 4 May, 1966.

The first person to orbit around the earth was Yuri Gagarin. He was launched into space by the USSR in 1961. He orbited the earth once and returned safely after 108 minutes. Valentina Tereshkova of the USSR was the first woman astronaut. In June 1963, she orbited the Earth 48 times and spent 2 days in space.

The longest runway in the world is at the Edwards Air Force Base at Muroc, California, USA. It is 11.9 kilometres long. Edwards Air Force Base is a landing site for the Space Shuttle.

The world's largest paper airplane had a wingspan of over 9 metres. It was built by pupils from schools in Hampton, Virginia, USA, in 1992. The plane was launched from a platform 3 metres high and flew a distance of 35 metres.

The US rocket-powered plane X-15 has set both speed and height records. It has reached a height of more than 100,000 metres. Its top speed is 7,274 km/h. A MiG-25 fighter holds the altitude record for a jet aircraft: 37,650 metres reached on 31 August, 1977.

Glossary

Aircraft Any machine which can fly. Balloons, gliders, airplanes and helicopters are all aircraft.

Airfoil (or **Aerofoil**) A surface, like an airplane wing, which is shaped to produce lift when air flows over and under it. The top surface of an airfoil is curved and the bottom is nearly flat.

Airplane (or **Aeroplane**) An aircraft with wings. Airliners are airplanes, but a hot-air balloon is not.

Altitude The height at which something is above sea level, or the height at which an aircraft flies. Modern airliners fly at an altitude of about 9,000 metres.

Aviation The operation of aircraft. People who fly aircraft are called aviators or pilots.

Elevator The part of an airplane's rear wing which causes the plane to ascend or descend as the pilot requires. On modern planes, the elevators are small flaps on the rear wings.

Jet engine An aircraft engine in which a stream of hot gases is forced out through an opening at the back of the engine. Most modern airliners use jet engines.

Lift The upward-acting force which stops an aircraft, whether it is a hot-air balloon or the Space Shuttle, from falling. In an airplane (an aircraft with wings), the force is produced when air flows around the wings.

Rotor The blades of a helicopter which rotate or turn. The main rotor of a helicopter produces a lift force.

Rudder The vertical flaps on the tail of an airplane which make it turn left or right, according to the pilot's instructions.

Thrust The force which drives an aircraft forward through the air. The thrust is produced by the aircraft's engine.

Turbine A set of blades like a windmill mounted on an axle. When gas or liquid flows through the blades, the axle rotates. Turbines are used in jet engines.

Turbofan A type of jet engine in which a fan at the front sucks air into the engine. Most modern jet aircraft use the turbofan engine.

Turboprop A type of engine which combines a propeller and a jet engine. Turboprop engines are not widely used today.

Famous Names In Aviation

Louis Blériot (1872-1936) French aviator who made the first powered flight across the English Channel in 1909. He began his career as a motor car engineer but turned to flying.

George Cayley (1773-1857) British inventor, now regarded as the 'Father of Aviation' because of his aircraft designs. He was the first to realize the importance of the forces (lift, drag and thrust) which act on an airplane.

Samuel Pierpont Langley (1834-1906) American engineer who built successful steam-powered model aircraft in 1896. His later attempts to build and fly a full-sized aircraft failed.

Otto Lilienthal (1848-1896) German pioneer glider builder who made thousands of flights and carefully recorded the results so that other aviators could make use of them.

Charles Lindbergh (1902-1974) American airmail pilot who made the first solo non-stop flight across the Atlantic in 1927 in the *Spirit of St Louis*. He also explored long-range air routes across the Pacific.

Etienne (1745-1799) and **Joseph** (1740-1810) **Montgolfier** French brothers who made the first hot-air balloon capable of carrying passengers in 1783. Papermakers from Annonay, near Lyon, their balloons were really large paper bags.

Alberto Santos-Dumont (1873-1932) Brazilian aviator who lived in Paris. He was the first person to achieve powered and sustained flight in Europe in his biplane in 1906.

Igor Sikorsky (1881-1972) Russian-born American aircraft designer. He built the first four-engined aircraft in 1913, and the first practical single-rotor helicopter in 1939.

Frank Whittle (1907-) British engineer who invented the basic design of the jet engine. In 1941 he built the first jet plane, the Gloster E28/39.

Orville (1871-1948) and **Wilbur** (1867-1912) **Wright** The American brothers who designed and built the first aircraft to achieve powered, controlled and sustained flight on 17 December, 1903.

Ferdinand von Zeppelin (1838-1917) German airship pioneer. His first rigid airship, the LZ1, flew for the first time on 2 July, 1900.

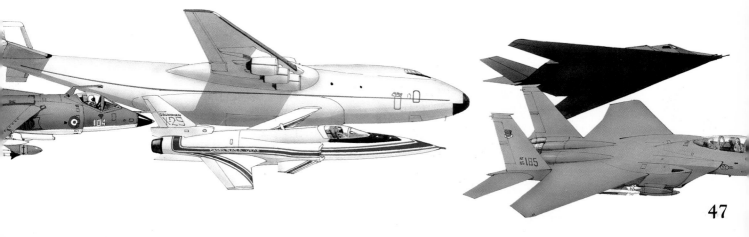

INDEX